COVERING DARKNESS

COVERING DARKNESS

Writing True Crime

NEIL ROOT

Greenwich Exchange
London

Greenwich Exchange, London

First published in Great Britain in 2019
All rights reserved

Neil Root © 2019

Printed and bound by imprintdigital.com
Cover design: December Publications
Tel: 07951511275

Greenwich Exchange Website: www.greenex.co.uk

Cataloguing in Publication Data is available from the British Library

Cover art:
(reproduced courtesy Shutterstock)

ISBN: 978-1-910996-22-5

for Tracy & Shana with Love

'Darkness cannot drive out darkness: only light can do that ... '
— Dr Martin Luther King Jnr

'Look at how a single candle can both defy
and define the darkness.'
— Anne Frank

CONTENTS

INTRODUCTION

'WHO READS STORIES OF TRUE CRIME? One imagines a furtive audience of sad saps and sadists, trench-coated lurkers and wan shut-ins.' Thus wrote Lorna Scott Fox in an article about true crime in *The Nation* in 2009. It's a mind-set familiar to many true crime writers when receiving slightly queasy reactions. 'I heard that you're a writer – what do you write about?' 'True crime.' 'Oh ... I see.' As in writing, less is more, and the shocked responses and slightly uneasy expressions speak volumes, with true crime considered by some as the embarrassing relative of the non-fiction family, on ethical grounds due to subject matter or lacking in literary merit due to accusations of sensationalism or a lack of style, both prongs of attack unfortunately sometimes legitimate, although a sweeping, simplistic and undiscerning generalisation. However, perceptions of the genre are changing slowly, as it has become more mainstream, and the increasing success of true crime documentaries, films, television dramas and podcasts have legitimised true crime narratives to a far wider audience.

In that same article, in which she reviewed Harold Schechter's seminal *True Crime: An American Anthology,* Lorna Scott Fox went on to acknowledge that many of the pieces included had real literary merit. This is a fact well known to those who really appreciate and understand the genre. Although like all genres, the quality of true crime prose covers a wide and varied range, from the fast-turnaround cash-in potboiler to the true work of art. This book, of course, focuses on the genre's best writing, and examines how the most masterly true crime writers have, and do, achieve real and lasting resonance and sometimes a deep connection with their readerships, for little can be more emotive than human tragedy, provided it is treated with care, and cheap tricks are not employed to manipulate.

It's also important and intrinsic to a real understanding of true crime to see how it has developed over centuries, and many may not realise just how many of the best and most respected writers – those considered to have written classics and passed the test of the tides of time rather than a fleeting impression of reputation forged in the sands of here and now – have written or dabbled in the genre. It's a truly impressive list of writers and journalists, those who have experimented with style and form, and sometimes made real innovations in prose writing. The creative imagination is often drawn to the dark, macabre and melancholy, and the extreme frontiers of the human mind and experience are excellent subject matter for writers who like to dig and mine deep.

So, what is true crime? The *Oxford Dictionary* defines it as 'a genre of writing, film, etc, in which real crimes are examined or portrayed.' The term was first used in the 1920s in the *Times*

Literary Supplement, but of course forms of the writing had been published long before that time, and the literary lineage and evolution of true crime are examined in these pages, along with the unique sensitivities and requisite skills and appraisals of fifteen practitioners, modern masters of the genre.

These authors take very different approaches to true crime, some reporting with total accuracy, others using a blend of fact and imagined colour, but both attempt to bring reality to life. There are writers of true crime books and feature articles, many masterworks, and all bonded by the high quality and serious intention of their writing. The writers chosen, whilst subjective – some readers may of course feel that a favourite has been omitted – represent the cream of true crime in modern times, which is usually defined in the genre as beginning in 1966 with the publication of Truman Capote's *In Cold Blood* and continuing right up to the present day.

These writers also display varied pathways to achieving what they set out to do with integrity whilst fearless in exposing uncomfortable and unsettling truths and sometimes horrors, the very best unflinching in this regard. This is also an ethical question – what should be included and what left out, what are the limits to the genre? As these writers will hopefully demonstrate, it's not what is included in the book so much as how the material is handled and the subject approached.

Perhaps the most widely debated aspect of true crime writing is the use of novelistic techniques to tell the story, pioneered by Capote in *In Cold Blood* and used many times since. How creative should true crime be before it veers off into the writer's imagination and away from the definition of the genre, the adjective 'true' being called into question, and accusations of self-indulgence made? True crime of course deals with real people and real tragedies, and the accuracy of their treatment can thus be highly controversial.

The veracity of Capote's reportage in a later true crime novella, *Handcarved Coffins*, was famously unmasked several years after his death by another writer included in this book, Peter Gillman, and years after that *In Cold Blood* itself was found to have many fictional elements. But novelistic techniques can be used to brilliant and insightful effect when used judiciously. There is a line to be drawn between fact and fiction in the genre, but that line falls differently to each individual reader. For all non-fiction writers, regardless of genre, only readers can make that final judgement.

TRUE CRIME

The Literary Lineage

THE TENTACLES OF TRUE CRIME CAN be traced back centuries, the reporting, re-creation and analysis of the criminal impulse having tantalised readers and the creative imagination of writers as far back as words were written down and distributed. The Bible and other seminal religious texts are rooted in human conflict or morality, immorality and amorality, and ethical questions focusing on extreme behaviour, its motivations and consequences are a fundamental intellectual impulse. Violence and murder especially have forever fascinated, but it was only in the latter half of the twentieth century that 'True Crime' was adopted as a label for the genre.

Joyce Carol Oates wrote in *The New York Review of Books* in 1999 that true crime 'appeals to the highly educated as well as the barely educated, to women and men equally.' This helps explain why the genre has attracted writers, of all qualities, from the most undiscerning to those of real literary excellence, through time – it sells when the subject matter or case covered chimes with current fears and preoccupations and is in tune with the zeitgeist. George

Orwell, that intellectually rigorous writer, was a fan of what became true crime, especially in newspaper form, commenting in his famous essay *The Decline of the English Murder.* 'It is Sunday afternoon ... The wife is already asleep in the armchair, and the children have been sent out for a nice long walk. You put your feet up on the sofa, settle your spectacles on your nose, and open the *News of the World.* In these blissful circumstances, what is it that you want to read about? Naturally, about a murder.'

Orwell was writing in 1946, and lamenting how the quality of British crime reporting in newspapers had declined, in his view, since before the Second World War. Reporting on crime had in fact been circulating narrowly and sporadically as far back as Elizabethan times in single crime-sheet form, and one only has to look at Shakespeare's oeuvre, especially *Hamlet* and *Macbeth*, to see how dark subject matter and moral conflict fascinated the public at that time. People have always liked to laugh and to be shocked, hence the Bard's comic and tragic veins. And Shakespeare, whilst considered by many as the consummate writer of the English language, was also commercially very shrewd, having to ensure that the Globe Theatre in London staged his plays once he'd penned them.

An early example of true crime reportage was *The Counterfeit Lady Unveiled* by Francis Kirkman, dating to 1673. As David Barnett points out in his 2017 article 'True Crime Pays: the History of Real-Life Crime Magazines', 'By 1714 there was a book available for sensation-hungry readers entitled *A Complete History of the Lives and Robberies of the Most Notorious Highwaymen, Footpads, Shoplifts and Cheats of Both Sexes.*' As the band The

Jam sang in a lyric to its 1980 song *Going Underground,* 'And the public wants what the public gets.'

It was in the early eighteenth century when real crimes as subject matter began to enter the mainstream via the printed word, focusing on famous trials and executions. The four-volume *State Trials* series first appeared in 1719, years before the far more famous *Newgate Calendar* began publication in the mid eighteenth century. *The Newgate Calendar* was assembled by 'the Keeper' of London's notorious Newgate Prison, and published monthly, until it appeared in book form in five volumes in 1773-4, a new edition coming out in 1824, proving so popular that an updated edition *The New Newgate Calendar* was published just two years later. The *Newgate Calendar* was the first 'true crime' in book form to humanise criminals to some extent – telling the story of their lives, but sanctimoniously focusing on the squalor, dissipation and immorality of their existence. By the 1860s, the *Newgate Calendar* would be published as more tabloid-flavoured 'Penny Dreadfuls' (illustrated magazine-pamphlets containing real crime and detective stories, along with crime fiction, often based on real-life crimes) which cost a penny and were highly sensationalised.

Back in the mid eighteenth century, major writers were also entering the early true crime arena, Henry Fielding being the first example. A jurist and magistrate in London, rising to Chief Magistrate, Fielding began as a playwright, writing numerous stage works with provocative titles such as *Rape upon Rape* (1730), inspired by an infamous rape case of the time, but actually an allegory which commented vociferously on political and judicial corruption in the English system. Fielding had in turn undoubtedly been influenced by the example of John Gay, whose *The Beggar's Opera* had premiered in London in January 1728, and became immediately popular. A three-act ballad opera, it was highly satirical, its targets being corruption of any kind, inequality, and comparing the criminal underclass with the higher echelons of society, the inference being that the privileged who controlled society were no better than those deemed villainous in the eyes of the ruling elite. Gay had been inspired by his friends, the satirical novelist and pamphleteer Jonathan Swift, and the satirical poet Alexander Pope. The use of allegory, parody and both subtle and scathing irony, to expose and comment on social injustice and the corrupt political system, as used by Swift, Pope and Gay, would soon infuse the work of Henry Fielding.

Fielding later became well known with his novels *The History of the Adventures of Joseph Andrews and his Friend Mr Abraham Abrams* (1742), later known simply as *Joseph Andrews* and *The History of Tom Jones – a Foundling* (1749), latterly known as *Tom Jones*, amongst many others, written in a satirical style. These were early examples of the English Picaresque novel, famously pioneered much earlier by Cervantes in Spain in the two volumes of *Don Quixote*, published in 1605 and 1615 respectively, although predated by the first English Picaresque novel – Thomas Nashe's *The Unfortunate Traveller: or, the Life of Jack Wilton*, which appeared in 1594.

But Fielding's interest in the plight of the poor and social justice was a continuing thread in his writing, and was shown in his fiction and in his work as Chief Magistrate, when he refused to take money from the very poor, calling this 'the dirtiest money upon earth', unlike many of those in that powerful position before and later, who fleeced the needy. Fielding's 1743 novel *The Life and Death of Jonathan Wild, the Great* is the closest that Fielding came to writing true crime in fictional form, using the scandalous case of London chief 'thief-taker' Jonathan Wild, self-dubbed 'Thief-Taker General', a criminal and early unofficial and self-appointed policeman before a force existed, who was enormously corrupt and who was himself hanged in 1725. Written in a sardonic and satirical style, the novel is nonetheless based on real fact, and set in the London underworld, which Fielding had come to know and understand well.

Henry Fielding and his brother John (who was already blind when he became Chief Magistrate after Henry's death in 1754 and known as 'the Blind Beak', but was able to identify criminals before him by their voices) would establish the Bow Street Runners in 1749, London's first semblance of a police force, the forerunner to the Metropolitan Police, which wasn't founded until 1829. Henry campaigned to have public executions abolished, seeing them as exploitative and immoral public displays, but interestingly he was not against the death penalty himself, once sentencing a criminal to hang, a robber and boxer named James Field in 1751, an Irishman who had moved to London and committed highway robbery with violence.

Henry Fielding was a devoutly religious man, and the power of God to overcome sin runs through his non-fiction writing about crime, as in the literal-titled *Examples of the Interposition of Providence in the Detection and Punishment of Murder* of 1752, which was a collection of over thirty murder cases in which Fielding claimed that 'this dreadful crime has been brought to light in the most extraordinary and miraculous manner, collected from various authors, ancient and modern.' In treatise form Fielding would also write a seminal work about social justice in that same year, *Proposals for Making an Effectual Provision for the Poor.*

By the late eighteenth century real crime articles were known as 'broadsides'. As Eric Linderman of Kent State University asserts in his 1997 mini-essay 'Criminal Broadsides of 19th-Century England', 'In the early nineteenth century, much of the news of England's murders and executions was brought to the masses through penny and half-penny broadsides. These papers were published by a number of printers in the Seven Dials neighborhood of London (presently Cambridge Circus). One of the most productive of these printers was James (Jemmy) Catnach, who produced broadsheets on Monmouth Street.'

By the 1830s these single-sheet broadsides sold by street-sellers were very common, telling true stories in prose, poetry and sometimes even in song lyrics, to be either read or sung, reporting on crime (especially murders), politics, religion and even shipwrecks, shocking readers, many little more than announcing a post-mortem examination or execution, the journalistic research undertaken very limited. A typical headline, from 3 May 1833, was ACCOUNT OF A MONSTROUSLY-CRUEL MURDER!!! – ON THE BODY OF AN UNFORTUNATE LADY NAMED MISS ELMS OF 17 WELLESLEY STR. NEAR THE NEW CHURCH, CHELSEA, ON THURSDAY NIGHT, OR FRIDAY MORNING LAST. A few years earlier there was the account of the execution of Margaret Harvey, 'a young woman of only 18 years of age, who was executed at the New Drop, London, on Monday the 8th of January, 1821, for the murder of her male bastard child.'

In 1827 the opium-addicted man of letters Thomas de Quincey published his essay 'On Murder Considered as One of the Fine Arts' in Edinburgh's *Blackwood's Magazine*, and a second definitive version followed in 1839. It was the first time that a renowned literary figure had taken crime as a subject in non-fiction form, focusing on the infamous London Ratcliffe Highway murders of 1811, with an attempt of the psychological analysis of the murderer John Williams and all those involved in that brutal case. De Quincey used methods in that essay which would be expanded on by true crime writers in the late twentieth century.

Beginning in the 1830s none other than Charles Dickens was also fixated on crime, his early-career *Sketches by Boz* including pieces about the Old Bailey and Newgate Prison. Then *Oliver Twist* was serialised by Dickens in the periodical *Bentley's Miscellany* between 1837 and 1839, and whilst it is one of the most famous British novels, it is based on real knowledge of London's underclasses, some of it personal from Dickens's own youthful experience in the workhouse. But *Oliver Twist* was also inspired by a real crime case.

In early December 2011 Rose Wild, the Archive Editor of *The Times*, came across a court report dated 14 January 1834, which documents the trial at Bow Street Court of 60-year-old Henry Murphy, a black man known as 'Old Murphy', who was in fact a child-stealer. The charge he faced was keeping a place for runaway children, who were forced to 'rob and beg for their suppers'. In 1834 Dickens was working as a political reporter for *The Times*, so he would have had easy access to that report. The first edition of *Oliver Twist* appeared four years later. The character of Inspector Bucket in *Bleak House* (1853) was similarly modelled closely on the real Inspector Field of the Metropolitan Police. Like many literary and crime novelists since, Dickens used real crimes and events to shape his fictional characters and plots. (Later literary examples are Theodore Dreiser's *An American Tragedy* and John O'Hara's *Butterfield 8*.) Over time crime genre novelists especially used reality as raw material, a logical practice which continues today, especially in long-running detective and police procedural book series.

Public executions were major public spectacles in early to mid Victorian England, and the novelist William Makepeace Thackeray wrote a piece in 1840 entitled 'Going to See a Man Hanged'. Dickens was a scaffold spectator too. On 13 November 1849 he attended the joint execution of Frederick and Marie Manning outside the Horsemonger Lane Gaol in Southwark, London, along with a crowd of some 30,000 people, and Dickens, by now wealthy from his writing, had even rented an upstairs room nearby for the occasion to give himself a good view. The couple had murdered a wealthy friend, Patrick O'Connor, for money and buried him under the floor of their kitchen. A contemporary broadside was published entitled *Life of the Mannings*. But Dickens himself was moved to write a letter to *The Times* on that very day after witnessing the executions:

> I was a witness of the execution at Horsemonger Lane this morning. I went there with the intention of observing the crowd gathered to behold it, and I had excellent opportunities of doing so, at intervals all through the night, and continuously from day-

break until after the spectacle was over ... I believe that a sight so inconceivably awful as the wickedness and levity of the immense crowd collected at that execution this morning could be imagined by no man, and could be presented in no heathen land under the sun. The horrors of the gibbet and of the crime which brought the wretched murderers to it faded in my mind before the atrocious bearing, looks, and language of the assembled spectators ...

Incredibly, Herman Melville, the American writer already with three novels to his name and the future author of *Moby Dick* and other classic works, was also in the crowd that day, unlike Dickens actually part of the throng, having paid half-a-shilling to witness the event. In his introduction to *True Crime: An American Anthology*, Harold Schechter recounts that Melville wrote in his journal on that trip to London, 'The mob was brutish. All in all, a most wonderful, horrible and unspeakable scene.'

Murder wasn't the only crime which got Charles Dickens's imagination sparking either. The character of Merdle in his 1857 novel *Little Dorrit* is a fraudster operating what would later be dubbed a 'Ponzi Scheme', killing himself when he knows that his crime has been detected. The character of Merdle was based on the real Irish conman John Sadleir, who had committed suicide in 1856, the year before Merdle entered the public literary world.

Wilkie Collins, the highly respected author of *The Woman in White* and other novels, was Dickens's contemporary, mentor, friend and occasional collaborator, and also fascinated by crime and criminals – Collins was a voracious reader of broadsides and court reports. His novel *The Moonstone* is considered by many the first modern detective novel in English, and the precursor and template of Conan Doyle's Sherlock Holmes, Christie's Poirot and Miss Marple and hundreds of other detective novels since. As Robert McCrum points out in his essay 'An Introduction to *The Moonstone*':

> In the 1920s, T.S. Eliot, claiming that the genre had been 'invented by Collins and not by Poe', declared it to be 'the first, the longest and the best of modern English detective novels'. Dorothy L. Sayers, a queen of crime in the 1930s and 40s, echoing Eliot, pronounced it 'probably the finest detective story ever written.' Its influence continues to animate the work of crime writers like P.D. James and Ruth Rendell.

The main detective in *The Moonstone* is Sergeant Cuff, whom Collins based on the real-life Detective Inspector Jonathan 'Jack' Whicher. He was one of the early Scotland Yard detectives (from the 1840s onwards). He was already famous for solving the murder of Constance Kent, a case re-examined and brought back to life in 2008 by Kate Summerscale in her bestselling true crime non-fiction book *The Suspicions of Mr Whicher or The Murder at Road Hill House. The Moonstone* also contains another character, Franklin Blake, who serves as a 'gentleman sleuth' in contrast to Cuff's (Whicher's) seasoned professional.

T.S. Eliot's assertion that Collins invented the detective novel in English and not Poe is, of course, a reference to Edgar Allan Poe, the hugely talented American gothic short-story writer and poet, who was also fascinated by real crimes. Poe's detective, C. Augustine Dupin, appeared in *The Murders in the Rue Morgue* (1841), *The Mystery of Marie Roget* (1842) and *The Purloined Letter* (1844), all short stories and works of fiction based partly on real cases, but with a large dose of Poe's unique and macabre imagination added.

The Moonstone is, in fact, arguably technically not the first novel in English featuring a detective, as Poe's Dupin predates Cuff by over twenty-five years, and Charles Dickens's character Mr Nadgett in *Martin Chuzzlewitt* (1843-4) is also awarded that honour by some. Also, a potboiler with a detective character entitled *Ruth the Betrayer* by Edward Ellis was published in London in 1863, five years before *The Moonstone*, although it was really nothing more than a penny dreadful. *The Moonstone*, while very simple in plot about the theft of a unique diamond, was the first novel which truly allowed the reader to see the plot unfold through the eyes of a detective, instead of through the furtive and nervous gaze of a criminal, and as such it is the first to use real detective work to a greater level of sophistication and reality in narrative form.

The great Russian writer Fyodor Dostoyevsky is one of the seminal novelists of the Victorian period, a writer of 'the Golden Age of Russian Literature' who used the themes of crime, murder, suffering (much of which he endured himself), original sin and the human condition in his work, in novels, novellas and short stories, in fact those themes are infused throughout his considerable output. Dostoyevsky mainlined crime and the criminal impulse, and he had real insight. The young Friedrich Nietzsche said that Dostoyevsky was 'the only psychologist from whom I had something to learn', although later Nietzsche thought that Dostoyevsky had become too messianic, and the religious and moral overtones of his work do increase over time, especially in his last novel, *The Brothers Karamazov* (1880). The great novels *Notes from Underground* (1864), *Crime and Punishment* (1866) and *Demons* (1872) utilise many of the skills of psychological analysis and human empathy which modern true crime writers attempt, and because of this, Dostoyevsky is a must-read for anybody interested in the genre.

In January 1889 Oscar Wilde published the great crime versus aesthetics essay 'Pen, Pencil and Poison' in the *Fortnightly Review*, which examined the life, art and motives of the artist, writer and poisoner Thomas Wainewright, who was a serial killer, although that term was far from coined then. Wilde wrote of Wainewright: 'His crimes seem to have had an important effect upon his art. They gave a strong personality to his style, a quality that his early work certainly lacked ... One can fancy an intense personality being created out of sin ... The fact of a man being a poisoner is nothing against his prose.' The case had also attracted the attention of Edward Bulwer-Lytton in his novel *Lucretia* (1846) and Charles Dickens in his story *Hunted Down* (1859). Oscar Wilde would, of course, famously return to the theme of crime, murder, motivation, sin and execution with *The Ballad of Reading Gaol* (written in 1897 immediately after his release from incarceration and published in 1898), which is undoubtedly the most well-known true crime-inspired poem in the English language.

After the journalist and editor W.T. Stead pioneered investigative reporting into crime just before the First World War, tabloid newspapers would increasingly focus on crime in their coverage, and cases such as Dr Crippen in 1912 would dominate front pages. The 1920s and 1930s were the period in which true crime truly became a public fixation in the newspapers, British tabloid newspaper circulations peaking in the 1950s, with crime stories a major reason for this spike. Reporting was sensational, and especially after the Second World War, often brutal in detail, leading to the crime coverage we see today in newspapers, magazines and on internet websites. Penny Dreadfuls would continue to be the main source of regular longer form true crime into the 1930s.

But in the mid 1920s, the bodybuilding American 'physical culture' and publishing magnate Bernarr Macfadden began publication of *True Detective* magazine, which started with fictionalised and licentious retellings of real crimes, but soon began publishing straight true crime, meaning journalistic reportage of real crimes. At its peak between the 1940s and 1960s, *True Detective* sold millions of copies every month. Macfadden added *Master Detective* to his portfolio, and there were many imitators, there being around 2,000 true crime magazines in the US by the early 1960s, after which they went into decline, as television became more popular. So while crime fiction writers such as Dashiell Hammett (a former Pinkerton agent himself who loved true crime), Raymond Chandler and Jim Thompson et al were writing short-stories for 'the pulps' beginning with *Black Mask*, there were magazines for crime journalists and true crime writers to sell their wares.

As regards the book form, William Roughead, a Scotsman, was one of the earliest true crime writers in Britain, publishing his first book *Rhyme Without Reason* in 1901. This was followed by many more books, the most influential perhaps being *The Trial of Oscar*

Slater (1910, revised 1925), which questioned the guilty conviction of Slater, a German immigrant, for an Edinburgh murder, and the conviction was later quashed in 1928. Henry James was reportedly an admirer of Roughead's true crime books, and his classical style of storytelling.

In 1905 an Edinburgh publisher began to publish the *Notable Scottish Trials* series of books, which each focused on one case – the first on the case of Madeleine Smith, a scandalous murder from 1857 in Glasgow, from which Smith was sensationally acquitted. The early true crime author F. Tennyson Jesse, and the first known female true crime author, wrote the introduction to that edition. Jesse was the grandniece of the former Poet Laureate, Alfred, Lord Tennyson, and became one of the most famous and respected true crime writers, both in journalism and book form, of the first half of the twentieth century. The *Notable English Trials* series began in 1911, and later, *Notable British Trials* in 1921. There would eventually be cheaper Penguin paperback editions covering several cases in each volume.

Former police officers on both sides of the Atlantic published memoirs about their careers and the cases they covered from the early 1920s onwards, at a time when many of these policemen were household names. The first in this true crime subgenre was Eugène Vidocq, a former criminal and founder of the French Police force, the Sûreté Nationale, who was also its first director. Vidocq had published his ghost-written memoirs in 1828, with writers of the calibre of Victor Hugo and Balzac being inspired by his life.

Herbert Asbury wasn't a policeman, but a journalist and crime historian who focused on the American underworld of the late nineteenth and early twentieth century, publishing books colourfully telling the story and evolution of the gangs of major cities and social epochs, such as *The Gangs of New York: An Informal History of the Underworld* (1928), *The Barbary Coast: An Informal History of the San Francisco Underworld* (1933), *The French Quarter: An Informal History of the New Orleans Underworld* (1936), *Gem of the Prairie: An Informal History of the Chicago Underworld* (1940), and *The Great Illusion: An Informal History of Prohibition* (1950).

Over in America distinguished journalists would often cover big trials for newspapers and magazines, producing long form true crime reportage, just as Rebecca West would later do in Britain with the trial of the Nazi Adolf Eichmann and other espionage cases, producing her important book *The Meaning of Treason*. But this form was pioneered in the US, examples being Damon Runyon, the author of *Guys and Dolls* and an authority on the New York underworld, covering the 1927 Ruth Snyder-Judd Gray case for Hearst Newspapers in New York, extending it into a far longer piece entitled *The Eternal Blonde* in a book in 1947. None other than the great iconoclastic journalist and literary critic H.L. Mencken wrote a scathing piece about the new liberal attitudes to, and folk-hero-worship of, the 'Public Enemy' violent criminals such as John Dillinger, Baby Face Nelson and Pretty Boy Floyd, called *More and Better Psychopaths*, which appeared in the *Baltimore Evening Sun* in December 1934. Another example is the literary novelist Elizabeth Hardwick, who wrote *The Trials of Caryl Chessman* in 1960 for *Partisan Review*.

But the real revolution in true crime came with the publication of Truman Capote's *In Cold Blood: A True Account of a Multiple Murder and Its Consequences* in 1966. Capote was already a highly acclaimed novelist, short-story writer and writer of reportage. He was the first truly literary writer to take a brutal real crime – the murder of an entire rural Kansas family by two petty hoodlums – and visit the scene of the crime, get to know locals and the police investigators, and then the killers themselves. It is an artistic masterpiece, and Capote claimed to have invented a new genre – the 'Non-Fiction Novel'. The book made true crime respectable to the mainstream, and opened up crime to many more serious writers as a subject. Conversely, the veracity of some of Capote's true crime reportage has been questioned and exposed as sometimes invented, a melding of fact and fiction in the case of *In Cold Blood*, and in the case of his later non-fiction novella *Handcarved Coffins: A Nonfiction Account of an American Crime* (1979), proven, by the British writers and investigative journalists Peter and Leni Gillman, to be almost wholly fictitious, although again extremely well written.

In Cold Blood has sold tens of millions of copies, and is the second bestselling true crime book of all time. The first is *Helter Skelter* (1974) by Vincent Bugliosi and Curt Gentry – a long book taking a ride into the hellish world of the murderous Charles Manson and his brainwashed followers, a subject that also inspired the journalist Gay Talese to write an excellent true crime feature for *Esquire* magazine in 1970, entitled 'Charlie Manson's Home on the Range', focusing on the ex-Western film-set ranch where Manson and his followers lived when they went on their terrible Los Angeles killing sprees.

Norman Mailer's *The Executioner's Song* (1975) was actually published as a novel, but used mountains of research and had the real killer Gary Gilmore, awaiting execution on death row, as its protagonist. The book won a Pulitzer Prize – the only true crime book to have done so. Other masterpieces in the genre would follow, and the best modern true crime writers, from Truman Capote onwards, are examined in the Modern Masters section of this book.

True crime had become a presence in every bookshop by the 1980s, and the release of the film *The Silence of the Lambs* in 1991, based around the fictional serial killer Hannibal Lecter created by Thomas Harris, spawned the seemingly undying true crime serial killer genre. In the second decade of the twenty-first century, true crime is enjoying a renaissance, with many dramatic films and television dramas and documentaries based on real cases. The internet has spawned true crime podcasts, which allow a case to be told in episodes. These first became popular with the Peabody Award-winning *Serial* (2014), created by Sarah Koenig, which now has multiple series, as well as many imitators. The true crime podcast is the newest true crime subgenre. True crime writing in books, feature articles, on television, film and on podcasts shows no signs of dying just yet.

ON WRITING TRUE CRIME

WRITING TRUE CRIME REQUIRES SKILLS USED in all forms of creative and journalistic writing, but when taken together as a whole writers require a unique skill set. This section examines that range of necessary skills, personally developed and identified through writing true crime and from wide reading within the genre. The final section of the book, Modern Masters, focuses on key writers of true crime and how they approach and achieve a very high standard of writing with these sensibilities. These five key skill areas can be abbreviated into an acronym: SPINS – **S**tory, **P**rotagonists, **I**nvestigation, **N**arrative and **S**ensitivities.

STORY

Choosing a viable and interesting story or case at the outset is, of course, imperative. If, as a writer, you are not curious, either intellectually, psychologically or emotionally in the crime to be covered, it will be much more difficult to write, especially in a longer form, and as in all forms and genres of writing, the best work emerges from the writer's total immersion in the story. If you have a fascination with the story or subject, the chances are that others, potential readers, will too. All professional writing is a mixture of writing for the target readership – knowing your readers and what they like – and writing for yourself, which doesn't mean self-indulgence, but having a real desire to know more and hopefully a preliminary handle on the story. Professionals sometimes have to force this process when commissioned, and it is always better when you are truly instinctively connected to the story, but in either circumstance, the writer has to 'find the way in'.

Gaining entry into the core of the story, finding the key motivation for the crime, is central when planning. A list of questions which come to mind in reaction to the case, linked to real people, who will be your 'characters', their backgrounds, how paths crossed, the location and atmosphere where most of the story or crime took place (always helped by a physical visit to that location) – all these questions and more should be asked. You are writing about real crimes, and the true crime writer, and his/her typical reader, must act as a detective, and evaluate both motive and opportunity for the crime(s). Some cases are far more complex than others, and sometimes this initial understanding takes time, involving the unravelling of conflicting angles. But this is essential. Once this has been achieved, and the writer is confident that they have a story which can be sustained over the length of a feature article or book, keeping the reader with them along the way and wanting to continue, you have your story.

Stories might be instantaneously reactive as was Truman Capote's circling of a tiny news item in the *New York Times* in

1959 about the murder of a Kansas farming family, which would lead to *In Cold Blood*. It could be a story from last night, a few months or years, decades or even centuries ago, but, of course, contemporary and recent stories require a different kind of research and investigation to historical true crime – the former needing much more on-the-ground investigation and interviewing, the latter more file and archive work, focused and relevant background reading vital to both. Making a timeline and a 'mind-map' of motivation and opportunity can be useful at the beginning, as visual prompts can enhance understanding and concentrate the mind. Once that first stage has been completed, the writer can focus on the key people who were identified while looking into the story.

PROTAGONISTS

The main people involved in your story, the protagonists, are obviously central to the action and the skeleton of your narrative, dictating the structure: what they did/didn't do or what was done/wasn't done to them. Whether you are focusing on an individual perpetrator or group of perpetrators, victim(s), investigators or witnesses, bringing these people to life is fundamental to lifting narrative. Writers of crime fiction have the pressure of inventing characters from nothing – although they almost always use real people and cases as a spur, mixing different qualities, characteristics, psychologies and foibles to create believable composite characters – whereas true crime writers have a readymade structure, the pressure comes from recreating those characters and their actions, for ethical and legal reasons as truthfully as possible. There is little or no legal comeback for the crime fiction writer, unless they fail to pixelate their composite character(s), leaving one of the inspirations easily recognisable and litigable. In the true crime genre, the literary stakes are far higher in this regard.

Motivation creates actions, and people – your protagonists – do those actions. The connection between motive and opportunity and the people doing those actions is often not clear, but takes real effort and deep lateral thinking to solve. Criminals of one sort or another will feature in true crime, and criminals by nature lie and obfuscate, unless they wish to be caught for the fame and twisted perception of glory. Things are often not what they first seem. The writer has to make a judgement, and decide how they are going to present that to the reader – by offering a balance, giving all the possibilities for the reader to decide, or taking a polemical approach if confident that this is why, where, when, how and what happened. It's usually best to be honest if you don't know the answer, despite doing the required research. Readers usually respect honesty, and this can often add to the mystery – let readers use their imaginations and work some things out for themselves. The old cliché 'less is sometimes more' really is true in this instance.

People close to protagonists, secondary and even peripheral characters also need to be brought alive, to different degrees obviously depending on their relevance. Motivation and opportunity often depend on those other people in your central characters' lives – if they are only empty cyphers the story can become uneven, everything invested in your protagonist(s), the rest of the human landscape blurred or blank. Good painters pay as much attention to the background behind their main subject as the main subject itself – the backdrop puts the main focus into much sharper relief, whether in a literary or visual sense. Writers paint pictures with words and the best strive for an even texture.

Detail is the key to good true crime characterisation, sometimes the tiniest morsel setting up a character. You work within the limits of fact, although some writers in the genre take a very novelistic approach and are more speculative, some irresponsible. This can be controversial, and since Capote published *In Cold Blood*, hailed as a non-fiction novel, the line between fact and fiction has been hotly debated, with many writers in the opinions of some crossing lines which should not morally be transgressed. True crime is, remember, by definition about real people and real crimes. The people drive the narrative, and you want to tell their stories as colourfully and with as much detail as possible, and this is achieved by genuine and determined legwork – deep research.

INVESTIGATION

Most true crime writing attempts to answer questions about a case, a crime or a criminal phenomenon. To truly understand, then structure and tell your story, the investigative stage, which will inform your narrative arc and the development of characterisation, must take place. That deeper level of detail can only be achieved by becoming a literary detective, and a plethora of journalistic skills will get you there.

Archive and file work, media scans of designated sources to make connections, scanning private letters and diaries if you are fortunate enough to have such access, time spent digging beneath the surface will make composition far easier. But the best true crime writers wear their research lightly. As Hemingway once used an iceberg to analogise a good clean prose style – the writing hinting at hidden depths but not showing everything – and Orwell spoke of good writing being 'clear and transparent, like a pane of glass', knowledge gained through investigation should be infused subtly throughout the narrative. Force-feeding of the reader and over-complication reduces fluency and can become patronising. Once again, less is more: filter your research through your narrative. This creates a cumulative power as detail builds upon detail and the mosaic of your story comes into the reader's view.

Key interviews are crucial, and ethical persistence is required (the Sensitivities section on p.42 deals with those ethics). Speaking to protagonists, a perpetrator or suspect, in or outside prison, guilty or perhaps innocent, even awaiting trial if the case is not thought prejudiced by long-term collaboration with a writer for post-trial publication, can be complicated. At the same time, the writer must avoid breaking the laws of contempt or sub judice, sensitively deal with the families of those accused or convicted, families of victims, and, in some cases, survivors.

Interviews should elicit as much detail as possible, with opening general questions being swiftly followed by several supplementary specific questions to drill deeper. But, of course, judgement and pragmatism are needed when conducting interviews, although your research and planning pre-interview should arm you there too. If your subject will agree to being recorded, a good Dictaphone or recording device with a USB function will enable quicker transcription later. The use of shorthand or the note-taking of key points is still useful though, as a guard against technological malfunction – you may not get a second chance to do the interview.

Background reading relevant to the case or phenomenon to further and consolidate understanding of the story can only be an advantage. However, when that reading has been intrinsic to the text, giving sources credit within the text or in footnotes and/or in bibliographical listing is recommended: showing the reader your own wide reading can only work in your favour, allowing the reader to invest more confidence in you. It is also respectful to your sources, and those who know the subject area can easily identify when an idea or argument has been lifted from elsewhere. Don't be afraid to wear your sources on your rolled-up sleeves – identifying the mental springboards that got you there increases your authority.

Finally, location is important to any story. The most accomplished true crime writers strongly evoke a sense of place, and this makes the story that much more powerful. You want the reader to get a real sense of the place where the crime occurred, your characters live or lived, and where your story is set. So visit the place(s) if at all possible – some writers have lived in their story's setting for months or even years, and making multiple visits during the investigation stage is common practice. Get involved and immerse yourself – the investment pays off in the end.

NARRATIVE

The narrative drives the story and choosing the correct approach before composition commences is, of course, a prerequisite. The arc of your story, like all stories, needs a beginning, middle and an end, but is it going to be chronological, a reverse narrative, flashbacks and fast-forwards (difficult to do well), or driven by your protagonists in separate sections, from their individual perspectives. Then there is the dialogue technique, when conversations are presented as in a play or film script. Repetition, tense shifts from past to present, and looping, returning themes, which link up at different parts of the story can also be highly effective, as can 'twist and turn' plot structures, as used in crime fiction, with red herrings a good way to focus the reader. But, as always, narrative approach should suit the story being told, and getting it right early on saves a great deal of time and effort later.

Selecting authorial voice is key: first person or third person – the first person 'I' is very rare and tricky to do well, a style favoured by New Journalism writers who broke through in the mid to late 1960s such as Tom Wolfe, Hunter S. Thompson and Gay Talese (the latter sporadically the writer of true crime), routinely did this, but in true crime it is a dangerous construct, as it makes the writer take prominence away from the victim(s) in the case. Should the true crime writer take precedence over those real people who suffered? If used, the first person 'I' is best used in a sardonic, self-deprecating way, and used liberally within this genre. The French writer Emmanuel Carrère used the first person 'I' expertly and to great effect in his true crime masterpiece *The Adversary*, and the way he did this is discussed in the Modern Masters section of this book, which follows.

The 'Camera Eye' technique, named and pioneered by the American writer John Dos Passos in his *USA Trilogy*, and expertly used by the great short story writer Delmore Schwartz amongst others, is a classic true crime narrative device. Letting the reader be the witness through the lens of your story, as if they are at the scene, can work very well indeed, if the sense of atmosphere is sufficiently invoked. Like a detective, readers are there with you all the way as the story unfolds, giving them as much control as you, as your narrative reveals itself little by little, until that sense of justice/injustice, denouement or cliff-hanger ending.

Then your style of prose, which is entwined with the formality of tone and register, is a formidable tool, and you really do need to make the right choice. For some of the best writers, there is no choice – they are stylists and instantly recognisable when they write. Others are constantly experimenting, and changing styles from project to project. Whether lyrical and poetic, sparse and pared-down, psychologically manipulative, deceptively dry and comic but with built-in shocks, or plainly written but intellectually slow-burning and thought-provoking or stunning – the writers examined in the Modern Masters section offer this full range of styles.

The primary function of narrative in true crime writing is to tell your story as effectively as possible, and whichever arc approach, authorial voice or style of prose chosen, it should be in service to that storytelling. Everything else is self-indulgent and, at worst, pretentious. Readers want a great story, told well, and narrative methods should fit the story, just as, in a perfect world, the punishment should fit the crime.

SENSITIVITIES
The ethical considerations of true crime are unique in writing, as

by its nature, the genre looks at traumatic or shocking events, from which there is almost always a victim or victims of one sort or another. As the title of this book says, you are covering darkness, and shadows are left on real people after negative events. So due care and compassion needs to be taken when dealing with real people, in how they are portrayed, and how interviewing is done and the results reported in the text. Not only is it unethical to abuse people's trust, especially the bereaved or those who have suffered, or untruthfully sully the memory of a dead victim in the pursuit of notoriety and sales, it is also damaging to the writer's reputation, and getting interviews and consequently into another story will be much more difficult. People really do 'vote with their feet', and the writer-subject relationship is usually based on trust.

That first approach is vital – the technique used by journalists of 'door-stepping', especially crime journalists (knocking on doors in the vicinity of a crime or where a protagonist lives or lived in the hope of gaining some juicy titbits) can only take you so far, and often nowhere at all. Sources need to be approached and cultivated gently, with frankness and honesty. Asking the appropriate questions at the right time and place is essential in opening up the subject, as is treating them with respect. It's of mutual benefit to both parties. That doesn't mean that searching questions cannot be asked – far from it – the aim of the interviews is to get those key answers, but how the questions are phrased, in what tone and when they are asked, taking into consideration the full implications of the subject's situation, is vital to good practice.

But it's important not just with the victims and their families and friends. Authors who engage with perpetrators or the accused also need to take care when working in the genre. Getting too close to a subject during collaboration isn't a wise move, and objectivity needs to be maintained if possible: warm relations, but not intimate friendships. Some writers weave their way into the trust of subjects, especially convicted criminals and accused suspects. Some say that those convicted of crimes, often heinous ones in the true crime genre such as murder, have lost their human rights just as their victims did. But is that really true in the hard light of conscience? The author Janet Malcolm, analysed in the Modern Masters section wrote a fantastic book looking into this question of the writer-subject relationship and the ethics of it.

The natural impulse of the non-fiction writer is to get to the truth, and this is exactly as it should be. True crime writing which doesn't at least try to establish some truth is not fulfilling the genre's potential. Writers have different levels of ruthlessness in getting the real story, and what is perfectly ethical to one can be deeply unethical to others, likewise with their readers. Readers need trust in the writer. What are the limits of what is right or wrong? This is subjective and every writer must find their own level. In truth, a very fine balance is required to achieve what is needed, and true crime writers particularly require this mixture of tenacity and ethics to do the job and do it well. This is one of the great difficulties of writing accomplished true crime.

MODERN MASTERS

THE FOLLOWING WRITERS HAVE BEEN CHOSEN as they represent the very best true crime writing, in both book and long-form feature article form. Ranging in time from the mid 1960s to the present day, what is considered as true crime's 'modern period', displaying all of the skills discussed in this book's previous section, each writer especially excels in different areas of that skill-set. To read these writers is both stimulating and informative, and a privilege for anybody with an interest in true crime.

JIMMY BRESLIN
Key Works
'Son of Sam' (newspaper column) 1977; extended version 1989
The Good Rat (book) 2008

Some true crime writers capture a milieu, a subculture, a way of life. Nobody did that better for the New York underworld than Jimmy Breslin, who died in March 2017. Born in Queens, New York City in 1928, Breslin began as a sportswriter and then turned to crime reporting, also working as a columnist for the last fifty years of his career.

In his columns Breslin focused on ordinary people and no more so than in his native New York. But an early column which set the template for Breslin's fascination with everyday people was his column from Washington in late 1963, when he was sent there to report on the funeral of the slain President John F. Kennedy. All the other journalists were focusing on Jackie Kennedy and the rest of the Kennedy family, the new President Lyndon B. Johnson and his wife Lady Bird Johnson, and visiting dignitaries. Breslin focused his reportage on Clifton Pollard, the gravedigger who dug the President's grave. After Breslin's column appeared, the rest of the press pack then besieged Pollard, Breslin having packed more meaning and emotion and capturing the shock and grief of the nation by his pen portrait of the man who gave Kennedy his last important service, than any of the other conventional reporting, and with Tom Wolfe, Gay Talese and Hunter S. Thompson, he was one of the key pioneers of what soon became known as the 'New Journalism'. It's little wonder that in 1986 Breslin received a prestigious Pulitzer Prize for Commentary, having continued to file excellent and unique columns for the next three decades.

But Breslin's fascination with, and knowledge of, the Mafia, especially the five Italian-American New York Families – Gambino, Lucchese, Bonanno, Colombo and Genovese – made him the city's go-to organized crime expert: Jimmy was known to have his acute ear to that dangerous ground. He drank in bars where 'made' Mafia men drank, knew real Godfathers, Capos and 'wiseguys', shylocks, armed robbers, loan-sharks and hitmen, and how the families worked together and 'rubbed' each other out in turf wars. Breslin was a walking encyclopaedia of Mafia lore and mores, a real crime journalist and writer who got involved, and got to know his subject, but always wore that knowledge lightly, often casually, in his writing.

The Mafia wasn't the only strong string to Breslin's bow, however. His fame led, in 1977, to an infamous serial killer writing to him at his New York paper, the *Daily News*. Breslin had been covering the random shootings of young people all over the city (eventually six dead and eight seriously wounded), by a lone gunman who craved attention and who wrote to the press calling himself 'Son of Sam', with demonic overtones, although the media had already dubbed him 'the .44 Calibre killer', due to his weapon of choice.

Having read Breslin's columns about the fear wrought by the pointless slayings amongst normal New Yorkers, the killer, an alienated loner and postal worker named David Berkowitz, who would eventually be arrested, wrote a taunting and sickening letter to Breslin in the middle of his rampage, which was duly published in his column on 5 June 1977. Breslin had informed and consulted the police, who sanctioned him publishing the letter in his column, which Breslin duly did, imploring the killer to give himself up. Sadly, Berkowitz claimed two more victims after Breslin's piece went out.

Breslin opened that column with a characteristically low-key 'We put the letter on the table and read it again.' This was in great contrast to the killer's opening line, which followed next in Breslin's column: 'Hello from the gutters of NYC which are filled with dog manure, vomit, stale wine, urine, and blood ... ' Breslin's column then relayed the whole story of the killing sprees, interspersed with reactions and dialogue from within his newspaper's offices, which heightens the power of the piece more – Breslin's speciality once again: juxtaposing the rational and normal with the irrational and abnormal, all told matter-of-factly and with a direct tone. Breslin draws you in to that sweltering hot New York summer of 1977, and you can smell and feel the fear enveloping the city before Berkowitz was finally taken in that August – not the glamorous late-seventies New York of Studio 54, but those seedy streets atmospherically portrayed in Paul Schrader's script for Martin Scorsese's 1976 film *Taxi Driver* – city streets that Breslin, and as his letter attested, the killer Berkowitz knew only too well.

Berkowitz signed off his letter to Breslin (whom he addressed as 'JB') referring to his victims, with 'In their blood and From the gutter, "Sam's Creation" .44', followed by a postscript telling the police to keep trying hard to catch him. Conversely, Breslin ended a later extended version of that day's column, published in book form in 1989, with 'Berkowitz pleaded guilty to six murders, and he was sentenced to 315 years in prison.' Breslin had the most striking contemporary true crime input on 'Son of Sam', and years later the final word on the case.

Breslin had a prolific output, but nowhere is his criminal knowledge and distinctive prose style more apparent than in his 2008 book *The Good Rat*. Written towards the very end of his long career, it offers his intensive and insightful knowledge and understanding of New York mob culture, distilled effortlessly in a highly readable manner. For just over two hundred pages the reader is transported into the inner workings of that underworld, a lifetime of observation and often first-hand interaction with that substrata of society displayed. Structured around the testimony of the Jewish gangster Burton Kaplan, who turned State's Evidence against other mobsters, and two corrupt and murderous New York cops who had carried out hits for Kaplan and his associates.

The book's opening is unforgettable and draws you straight into that world. 'What I'm doing, I'm kissing the mirror, and I'm doing it so I can see myself kissing and get it exactly right, no tongue and no fucking slop. This way I can go into the clubhouse and kiss them on the cheeks the way I'm supposed to. That's the Mafia. We kiss hello. We don't shake hands. We kiss.' That encapsulates the hubris of the Mafia, the uber-masculinity which is close to, or crosses over into, homoeroticism.

Breslin knew and professionally engaged with that world, but never excused the immoral and shameful actions of those mobsters. He observed as a criminal sociologist, as the best true crime writers do. He understood the culture, but didn't agree with it. But neither was he sanctimonious about that culture. He knew that it was just a fact of life – the reader subtly knows that he doesn't approve of it from his tone, giving the impression, and once or twice directly saying, that mobsters end up either dead or in prison, but he allows the reader to make their own judgement.

Along the way, we are introduced to legendary mob figures such as John Gotti, Joey Gallo, Sammy 'the Bull' Gravano, Anthony 'Gaspipe' Casso and Jimmy Burke, who Robert De Niro played in the film *Goodfellas*, which was based on the true crime book *Wiseguy* by Nicholas Pileggi. Breslin often drank with Burke in a bar called Pep McGuire's and was on friendly terms with him, but this relationship came under strain in the late 1970s when Breslin divulged inside details of the 1978 $5.8 million Lufthansa robbery at New York's JFK airport, which was depicted in the film *Goodfellas* and Burke masterminded in real life. Breslin tells us that Burke 'plotted it from his room in a halfway house, the Hotel Breslin, on Broadway in Manhattan. Of course, they stole my name.'

But Burke forgave Breslin later, and even offered to pay for cancer treatment for Breslin's then wife. Jimmy Burke would never do time for that heist or any of the murders committed immediately afterwards to silence associates, but would eventually technically go to prison for fixing a college basketball game, but everybody knew, Breslin tells us, that the Brooklyn prosecutor wanted to nail Burke at any cost.

Breslin is also very funny at times, and this dry humour makes the violent actions described in his writing all the more shocking sometimes. When describing the atmosphere in the courtroom as his protagonist Burton Kaplan gave evidence for the prosecution, and whether it would be truthful, Breslin quotes some evasive testimony given by a Chicago hoodlum in a similar situation decades earlier:

Q. 'Do you know Al Capone?'

A. 'No.'

Q. 'You don't?'

A. 'No.'

Q. 'I show you this picture. Who is in the picture?'

A. 'Me and Al Capone.'

Q. 'You just said you didn't know him.'

A. 'I met him. That don't mean I know him.'

Q. 'What does Mr. Capone do for a living?'
A. 'He told me he sold ties.'
Jimmy Breslin was a class act.

GORDON BURN
Key Works
Somebody's Husband, Somebody's Son (book) 1984
Happy Like Murderers (book) 1998

Few writers are greatly respected amongst their peers and also achieve wide public recognition in their lifetime. Gordon Burn was one such writer and the sheer breadth of his output, in both non-fiction and award-winning fiction, combined with a truly powerful and insightful prose style, a very fine ear for dialogue and dialect, all backed up by immense primary research, have very rarely been equalled. In true crime, he was additionally very adept at mixing mundane, everyday detail with actions of extreme depravity, without flinching, or sensationalising nor trivialising those actions.

His first book, *Somebody's Husband, Somebody's Son* (1984), the true story of Peter Sutcliffe, the Yorkshire Ripper, is widely regarded as a masterpiece. Burn moved to Bingley, outside Bradford in Yorkshire for two years, and got first-hand interviews with Sutcliffe's family and people who had known him, in the wake of massive tabloid interest, which was quite a feat – arguably only matched by Truman Capote's magnum opus *In Cold Blood.* In his book Burn displayed the compassion and psychological insight, which along with his crystal smooth prose style, would become hallmarks of both his fiction and non-fiction. Of *Somebody's Husband, Somebody's Son*, Norman Mailer said 'A book which will with some justice be compared to *In Cold Blood* and *The Executioner's Song* ... It is as if Thomas Hardy were also present in the writing of this account.' Patricia Highsmith said that 'We come to know all these people as we might characters in a novel, and the book picks up a narrative current that keeps the reader turning the pages.'

The opening of *Somebody's Husband, Somebody's Son* is a master-class in narrative scene and atmosphere setting, placing Peter Sutcliffe in his Yorkshire roots: 'Although less than six miles along the Aire valley from Bradford, the enduringly Victorian "Worstedopolis" whose dormitory it has increasingly become, Bingley is in many ways a country town, distrustful of, and often hostile to, what are all too easily interpreted as slick city ways ... ' He goes on to describe how Mrs Gaskell, when travelling in the locality in early Victorian times, was 'immediately struck by the sullen and suspicious demeanour of the people ... ' Towards the end of the book, Burn reports, from an interview with Peter's brother Carl, how Sutcliffe, now in prison, explained his multiple murder and mutilation of women to his brother: 'Asked why he had done it, Peter had looked at Carl, and smiled, and said, "I were just cleaning up streets, our kid. Just cleaning up the streets."' In many ways a classically written book, Burn's approach to his macabre subject was novel and ground-breaking, the detail breath-taking.

In the mid 1990s, after an interlude writing fiction, Burn returned to true crime non-fiction with *Happy Like Murderers* (Faber, 1998) the story of the depraved serial killers Fred and Rosemary West who buried their victims in their 'House of

Horrors', 25 Cromwell Street, in Gloucester, England. Burn attended the famous West trials along with other leading crime writers, two of whom, Duncan Campbell and Brian Masters, are also profiled in this book. This time, Burn began from a survivor's viewpoint, and he invented a new prose style where themes gradually dig into the reader's psyche through repetition and convergence, worming deeply into the reader's consciousness.

Take this description of the voyeuristic serial rapist and mass murderer Fred West's twisted mind: 'He would dedicate the remainder of his life to his lust to look and his need to explore orifices and holes. Holes in his house which he packed with the headless and legless torsos of girls and young women: he said he "always wanted the body to fit the hole". And the bodily holes of his wife and other women and girls ... ' At the end of that section, Burn wrote, ' "We've found another hole," said Mr Bennett, the policeman in charge of the search for bodies inside 25 Cromwell Street would say whenever another body was found.'

Tackling a very difficult subject, Burn managed to write with compassion about the Wests' victims and was able to bring their sordid tale into some measure of reality, echoing Hannah Arendt's phrase about 'the banality of evil', although the toll on the author was large, Burn reportedly almost suffering a breakdown. Whilst Burn was writing *Happy Like Murderers*, he also wrote a deeply incisive essay, 'The Trial', about the media representation of murder, published in *Granta*, and this is fascinating as to Burn's thinking as he was writing the book, the tantalising opening line reading 'There are constants in the media landscape, the images that, even half-seen, alert us to another excitingly dire occurrence

... ' Like *Somebody's Husband, Somebody's Son, Happy Like Murderers* truly rewrote the rules of true crime, and meant that Burn produced two masterpieces in the genre.

DUNCAN CAMPBELL
Key Works
That Was Business, This Is Personal (book) 1990
The Underworld (book) 1994
A Stranger and Afraid: The Story of Caroline Beale (book) 1997
We'll All Be Murdered in Our Beds (book) 2016

When Britain needed a true crime writer and journalist to match Jimmy Breslin, it was given Duncan Campbell. Born in Scotland in 1944, Campbell had a spell as a copywriter in a major advertising agency before going travelling and turning to journalism in 1971. After noteworthy spells at the *London Daily News, Time Out* and *City Limits* magazines and a London radio station, Campbell was established as a crime writer of repute, and covered some major murder cases of the 1970s and 1980s. Between 1987 and 2009 he was a Senior Reporter and a correspondent for the *Guardian*, working out of the London headquarters, although for a time he was the newspaper's Los Angeles correspondent. Campbell is now a freelance journalist and writer and still regularly publishes articles, crime novels, and true crime non-fiction.

Campbell is both a crime and media expert, and as an ex-Chairman of the Crime Reporters' Association, there is little he doesn't know about the subject or the industry, and has worked alongside some of the very best journalists of his generation, and the one before and after, which enabled him to write his comprehensive history of British crime reporting, *We'll All Be*

Murdered In Our Beds. But like Breslin, Campbell is relaxed about his knowledge, and as the old adage goes, has probably forgotten more than many other crime writers know. He has also always been a writer who gets out there, and again like Breslin, his long journalistic career meant that he had to get the story.

From interviewing the infamous and murderous London gangsters the Kray twins, Ronnie and Reggie, in Broadmoor Mental Hospital for the Criminally Insane and a maximum security prison respectively – the diagnosed-as-insane Ronnie turning to Campbell at the end of one interview and saying 'You won't say I'm mad will you Duncan? They all say I'm mad ... ' – to a cast of other British underworld 'faces', to menial drug pushers and street operators – to other killers, triggermen and leading lawyers, armed robbers, cat burglars and master cracksmen, senior and junior police officers and fraudsters, Campbell has reported on, and written about, most areas of crime. His first book, *That Was Business, This is Personal: The Changing Faces of Professional Crime* displays a vast array of criminal contacts, on both sides of the law, and they all agreed to be interviewed, no mean feat. This shows the respect and trust in which Campbell is held.

The book provides an amazing insight into the motivations and thought processes of criminals and those who chase, catch, prosecute and defend them. No other book gives you such insights, straight from the source. Campbell passes no judgements, just introduces the subjects and lets them talk. It's a rare opportunity to rifle through a leading crime journalist's contact book and to see what the names inside really have to say. And they opened up to Campbell, the result being a truly important document of late twentieth-century British true crime, covering all levels of the hierarchy, and from all sides. Take this about the late Charlie Richardson, the leader, along with his brother Eddie, of the infamous south London Richardson gang, chief rival to the Krays in the 1960s, before they went down at the sensational 'Torture Trial' in 1966, as they had allegedly tortured gangland opponents and associates: 'Charlie Richardson, he of a couple of ages back in criminal history, is now a City businessman, having served eighteen years of that twenty-five year sentence. He looks the part – smart, well-cut suit, neatly trimmed beard ... "The City is much more crooked than anything I was ever involved in," he said.'

Campbell's 1994 book *The Underworld* was also a major BBC series, and delves into the different facets of crime from the turn of the twentieth century through to the early 1990s. Every possible area of criminality is covered, and some of the characters are more fascinating than any in crime fiction. For example, Campbell secured long interviews with the legendary cat burglar Peter Scott, who was operating in London in the 1950s and 1960s, robbing the rich, one of his victims being the Italian actress Sophia Loren. Campbell writes: 'His [Scott's] informants included chauffeurs from Knightsbridge (an exclusive area of London) who let him know the addresses of the wealthy and when functions were being held. Scott was modest about his skills. "The term cat burglar has been romanticized. You're really only a dishonest window cleaner. I actually watch window cleaners doing much more dangerous things than I've done."'

To those who know something about British true crime, it's astonishing how many times in *The Underworld* that Campbell gives over privileged, exclusive information not yet known to the public at that time. He does this with no fanfare, just integrates it into the text – there's no 'I can exclusively reveal', or 'It can be exclusively revealed'. Campbell gives the reader more than most true crime writers, imparts his knowledge generously, and this puts him a cut above many other chroniclers of British true crime, and does it with a fluid and muscular prose style which is often infused with irony, very fitting for true crime, for often events and motivations are superbly ironic. Campbell's the real thing, and one of the very best true crime writers and journalists that Britain has produced.

TRUMAN CAPOTE
Key Works
In Cold Blood (published in serial form in the *New Yorker* September-December 1965; book 1966)
Handcarved Coffins (book) 1979

The publication of *In Cold Blood: A True Account of a Multiple Murder and its Consequences* in 1965-66 ushered in the modern period of true crime. It really was that ground-breaking. As we have seen in the Literary Lineage section, some very distinguished writers had written within the genre for many years, but Capote was the first time a truly first-rate writer, or literary 'artist' (as he liked to call himself with some justification), had taken on a crime and focused on it in book-length long-form, and raised the treatment of it to high art.

Even the highly competitive Norman Mailer (who like Hemingway was rarely complimentary to fellow scribes) and who was Capote's long-time acquaintance and professional rival, once said that Capote was the 'most perfect' writer of his generation, and his prose style was extraordinary, possessing real beauty, with a natural rhythm and each word earning its place, every one of those words doing a great deal together, but individually not seeming to be doing anything at all, so fluent and even is it – there are no 'joins' in Capote's writing, just a smooth finish.

Capote had, of course, already established himself as one of America's best writers by 1959 when he saw the tiny report in the *New York Times* about the brutal murders of the entire Clutter family out in the rural Midwest in Kansas. His novels and most recent, now classic, novella *Breakfast at Tiffany's* had received great critical acclaim, and he was already a very visible media presence to American TV viewers. In the 1950s Capote had written long-form and book-length non-fiction too, also to great accolades and there seemed little that the diminutive but razor-tongued Capote couldn't do in writing – he had a wide range of skills, and those were of the highest calibre.

Capote later said that he had been looking for a true subject to engage with over book length, to see what he could do, as he wanted to meld his considerable novelistic and reportage skills together, in what would become known as the 'Non-Fiction Novel', although contrary to belief, Capote never claimed to have invented that genre. Other writers had utilised it before, most notably Lillian Ross with her long-form piece, *Picture*, which focused on the filming by John Huston of Stephen Crane's *The Red Badge of Courage* in 1950 and used a novelistic style to bring that set to life – skills later developed through the New Journalism movement in the 1960s.

Capote researched heavily for *In Cold Blood*, staying in down-at-heel motels in Holcomb, Kansas, first visiting there with his childhood friend and fellow writer Nelle Harper Lee, who was soon to publish her classic novel *To Kill a Mockingbird*. She was integral to Capote getting an 'in' with the locals, who were suspicious of him, a city slicker 'swell' who was eccentric to them in both manner and appearance. Capote cultivated a close relationship with the main policeman on the Clutter murders case, and this opened up the wider community to him. Later, after their arrest – Capote was truly on the scene as the search for the killers was in action.

When they were finally arrested, Capote also befriended them: Perry Smith and Dick Hickock, farm invaders who had needlessly and brutally murdered a father, mother, daughter and son. Capote would later claim that this closeness to the killers (particularly Smith) whom – spoiler alert – he would later watch being hanged, had taken a great emotional toll on him. Capote was ruthless on himself, as well as on his subjects. He was a writer in every sense, his identity and sense of self irrevocably entwined with his art.

His later descent into deep personal demons, ostracism from his high society circles after transparently portraying famous members of that set in his unfinished novel *Answered Prayers* (explosive chapters of which were published in *Vanity Fair* magazine), amphetamine and alcohol abuse, which would lead to his premature death in 1984, could all have been linked to the emotional torments he carried after composing *In Cold Blood*, or perhaps just a murky path that riches and extreme fame, together with his addictive personality, took him. But Capote even said in a late interview in the early 1980s with Lawrence Grobel about *In Cold Blood*, 'Well, I certainly wouldn't do it again. If I knew or had known when I started it what was going to be involved, I never would have started it, regardless of what the end result would have been.'

But the writing and narrative drive is nothing short of exemplary. Take the way the book opens: 'The village of Holcomb stands on the high wheat plains of western Kansas, a lonesome area that other Kansans call "out there". Some seventy miles east of the Colorado border, the countryside, with its hard blue skies and desert-clear air, has an atmosphere that is rather more Far West than Middle West.' Immediately we are in those open, elevated, endless fields, feeling isolated and somewhat alien, a stranger in a place that is home to many, but not us. But Capote takes us there, expertly, succinctly and stylishly.

Examples of Capote's consummate scene setting and atmosphere-building are evident on most pages of his masterpiece. An example randomly taken is his description of the bedroom of one of the murder victims, sixteen-year-old Nancy Clutter, on the Clutter farm. 'Nancy's bedroom was the smallest, most personal room in the house – girlish, and as frothy as a ballerina's tutu.' Or his opening portrayal of her murderer, Perry Smith, comparing his habits to one of his victims. In this scene, Perry is waiting for Dick Hickock to come and pick him up prior to the murders: 'Like Mr Clutter, the young man breakfasting in a café called the Little Jewel never drank coffee. He preferred root beer. Three aspirin, cold root beer, and a chain of Pall Mall cigarettes – that was his notion of a proper chow-down.' Capote is masterly at evoking character, in all his protagonists, whether it's the tragic murder victims, their killers, or the lead detective on the case, Alvin Dewey. He doesn't skimp detail on peripheral characters, giving his narrative a steady power.

The publication of *In Cold Blood* broke the mould and offered true crime a new respectability, one that it had hitherto not enjoyed. Serialised first in the, by then, somewhat elitist *New Yorker*, it gained a wide literary audience before it became a mainstream bestseller, and has now sold tens of millions of copies – it had sold around fifteen million copies by the early 1980s alone – not bad for an intrinsically literary book. It also became a core text taught on journalism courses, and every serious new true crime book is still immediately compared to it, over half a century after it was published. Capote interviewed other murderers in prisons after 1966, including Charles Manson's murderous follower Bobby Beausoleil, about whom Capote wrote an insightful piece, revealing that he thought that Beausoleil was the true mastermind behind the brutal 1969 Los Angeles Manson killings, and not Charlie Manson himself.

Capote didn't return to long-form true crime until he published the novella *Handcarved Coffins: A Non-Fiction Account of An American Crime* in 1979, which was exposed as almost totally fictitious by the leading British investigative journalists Peter and Leni Gillman (profiled in this section) in their legendary long feature *Hoax*, published eight years after Capote's death. In 2013 others finally followed the Gillmans' lead, and revealed that sections of *In Cold Blood* had also been invented. Capote might well have defended himself by saying that it was artistic license, and that true artistic talent must be given a free rein. But Capote had certainly been disingenuous about *In Cold Blood*, and truly dishonest about the veracity of *Handcarved Coffins*, which, in literary terms, is a wonderful and evocative piece of writing and a minor masterpiece itself. Capote's reputation and pedigree as a researcher and trustworthy true crime chronicler has consequently been tarnished in the eyes of some.

But Capote's writing artistry cannot be in question – he is a major writer, one of the very best of the twentieth century, and his contribution, impact and influence on the true crime genre is undeniable, if now qualified. Perhaps the best epitaph for Capote is the one used by Lawrence Grobel in the dedication to his book *Conversations with Capote*: 'For Truman, who sharpened his pencils and wasn't afraid.'

EMMANUEL CARRÈRE
Key Works
The Adversary (book) 2000 (original French edition *L'Adversaire*)

One of the leading French writers of his generation, Carrère, who was born in 1957, writes fiction, often with dark themes, and non-fiction. *The Adversary* is, so far, his only venture into true crime, and it's a masterpiece.

It is the true story of a Frenchman, Jean-Claude Romand, who murdered his wife, children and his parents in their homes in eastern France, close to the border with Switzerland and over that border respectively, to stop them finding out about his double life, and the empty truth of his personality and existence. Romand was seemingly a doctor, but also a Walter Mitty character who hoodwinked his family and friends for years into believing that he was a high-flying researcher at the World Health Organisation. In fact, he had dropped out of medical school and never qualified as a doctor, unbeknown to those closest to him. He had no job, at least hadn't for a long time, was an adulterer, massive debts had mounted, and all was about to be exposed. Romand had kept up his vast spider-gram of lies for eighteen years, and his fractured personality and narcissistic ego could not face that exposure.

Carrère wrote to Romand in prison in the early 1990s, attended his trial in 1996, and watched him jailed for life, although in fact he is now eligible for parole. Visiting the scene and area of the murders, interviewing close friends and getting a real feel for Romand's life, Carrère instils the sense of ordinary, sedate surroundings, in the midst of which lies this incredible imposture, culminating in Romand's psychological disintegration and the monstrous acts he committed to keep his internal fantasy life intact.

The book's opening sentences take us straight into that juxtaposition of the normal and abnormal, Carrère using himself and his own life in Paris as narrator to starkly show us that. It is one of the great true crime openings:

> On the Saturday morning of January 9, 1993, while Jean-Claude Romand was killing his wife and children, I was with mine in a parent-teacher meeting at the school attended by Gabriel, our eldest son. He was five years old, the same age as Antoine Romand. Then we went to have lunch with my parents, as Jean-Claude Romand did with his, whom he killed after their meal.

This double thread seams throughout the book, and the dual identity of the perceived Jean-Claude Romand and the hollowness of his reality create a constant tension. It's written to a perfect length, the liquid prose runs fast, but at the end of paragraphs, and indeed the end of the book, you need time to think and breathe. Carrère takes us up close and personal to what had been the fraudulently personable Romand's life and all those believers surviving within it, and then into the horror and narcissistic personality disorder behind that charade, which led to that terrible, shuddering climax. Carrère is an extremely powerful writer, and he forces us to confront our sense of humanity through Romand's inhuman acts.

DOMINICK DUNNE
Key Works
Justice: Crimes, Trials & Punishments (book) 2001

Dunne, who died in 2009, had been a successful Hollywood producer and a novelist before turning to writing true crime, specialising in murder and corruption within American high society and amongst the wealthy which brought a unique perspective to true crime – his own daughter, Dominique, an actress who most notably had appeared in the horror film *Poltergeist*, was murdered by her ex-boyfriend, a chef at the celebrity LA restaurant Ma Maison, a haunt of Hollywood stars including Orson Welles, in 1982. Dominick Dunne attended the trial, and when his daughter's killer was convicted only of manslaughter and received six-and-a-half years in prison, an enraged Dunne wrote a searing feature article about the case and trial, which was published in *Vanity Fair* magazine.

It was his entry into the genre, and he became synonymous with *Vanity Fair*, to which he became a kind of 'special' writer.

But his articles are far from mere frothy entertainments – there is a powerful brain behind them, a sense for the need for justice and a desire to examine and expose the unjust advantages afforded the rich and privileged, a world which he truly understood. For that, and his fluent facility in narrative, Dunne's work is both important and highly readable.

His best pieces for *Vanity Fair* over almost twenty years were collected in *Justice: Crimes, Trials & Punishments*. The book represents the very best of his output and Dunne covered almost all the major 'celebrity' American trials of the 1980s and 1990s, including that of the murder of Vicki Morgan, the mistress of Alfred Bloomingdale of the department store dynasty, and the trials and acquittals of Claus Von Bülow and O.J. Simpson respectively. But Dunne's best feature article is arguably *Nightmare on Elm Drive*, his analysis of the case of the Menendez brothers, the rich Los Angeles siblings who brutally murdered their parents to gain control of their $14 million inheritance while young, although they claimed at trial that they had been both sexually and emotionally abused by their father.

Dunne says in his afterword to his piece in *Justice: Crimes, Trials & Punishments* that he became 'deeply and personally involved in this story.' There was no need to tell us that. Dunne couldn't speak to the arrested brothers themselves, as it was pre-trial, and Erik's fearsome celebrity lawyer, Leslie Abramson, whom Dunne expertly profiles, would never have allowed that. But he spoke to almost everybody else who mattered in the case, to people who knew the brothers well, and those who were witness to what they had been doing since the murders. It shows.

Dunne begins *Nightmare on Elm Drive* by placing himself at the centre of the narrative, recounting a random meeting on a plane flight where he got talking to a teenage boy seated next to him, who lived in a prestigious street in Beverly Hills, Los Angeles. Lyle and Erik Menendez had been arrested for murdering their parents just a week earlier, and the media was ablaze with the story. Dunne knew Beverly Hills well, having once been involved in the film industry. The street where the boy lived was very similar to, and in the same area as, Elm Drive, where the Menendez family lived, and where two of them, José and Kitty, died very unnatural deaths. Dunne asked the boy if he had known the Menendez brothers, and the boy hadn't, as they were a few years older than him. 'A terrible thing,' said Dunne about the murders. 'Yeah,' replied the boy, 'but I heard the father was pretty rough on those kids.' This sets the template for Dunne's forensic examination of the crime and the protagonists within it.

The Menendez case is psychologically a fascinating one, and Dunne goes deeply into it. What could cause two young men, Lyle aged twenty-two and Erik nineteen, to facially obliterate their parents, shooting their father five times with a shotgun, then spending nine cartridges on their mother. Dunne is very adept at giving the reader an insight into the world about which he is writing. Here he talks about the Menendez home, and it tells us that the murdered patriarch José Menendez, a man who had worked himself up from nothing to be a top entertainment executive, was more interested in appearances than realities. 'Like a lot of houses of the movie nouveau riches still in their social and business rise, the grand exterior is not matched by a grand interior.' Dunne has just defined the sensibilities of Hollywood in one sentence.

Here's Dunne describing the inside of the Menendez mansion, which he gained access to after the arrests of Lyle and Erik. 'Every person who saw the death scene has described the blood, the guts, and the carnage in sick-making detail. The furniture I saw in that room was replacement furniture, rented after the murders from Antiquarian Traders in West Hollywood. The original blood-drenched furniture and Oriental carpet had been hauled away, never to be sat on or walked on again.' Dunne goes on to imagine what happened on the night of the murders, which took place in the living room, looking at every perceivable possibility, as if we, the readers, were inside the minds of the investigating detectives at the crime scene. By the end of this lengthy feature article, Dunne has humanised the Menendez brothers and their previous lives, but forces no judgement as to their guilt, or whether there really were mitigating factors of terrible familial abuse behind the commission of the murders. He gives us the facts, as far as he could pre-trial and sub-judice, and then like every quality true crime writer, he lets us make up our own minds.

PETER & LENI GILLMAN
Key works
'Hoax: Secrets that Truman Capote Took to the Grave' (feature article) 1992
'Exclusive: Moors Murderer Ian Brady's Childhood' (feature article) 2005
'Harry Horse: The Man Who Loved His Wife to Death' (feature article) 2008

Writing and researching teams in true crime are rare, and a married team is almost certainly unique. But Peter and Leni Gillman are seasoned investigative journalists and writers, who have produced award-winning narrative non-fiction books on mountaineering, and definitive biographies of the Everest pioneer George Mallory and the rock star David Bowie, as well as significant contributions to the true crime genre.

Leni is a former teacher, and like Peter, an accomplished writer and journalist. Peter, who gave Gordon Burn his first journalistic break at the beginning of the 1970s, when Gillman was the features editor of the *Radio Times*, then went on to freelance on the *Sunday Times*, before becoming a staff member, working on the then legendary *Insight* investigative unit of that paper until the early 1980s. He rose to deputy editor, breaking major stories and taking part in seminal, complex and long-running investigations, in the days when Lord Thomson was the proprietor, and funding for important journalism was adequate, mostly under the editorship of probably, journalistically, the best newspaper editor that Britain has ever produced, Harold 'Harry' Evans.

Having worked as a freelance team since then, as well as training journalists, Peter and Leni Gillman have published seminal feature articles on varied subjects, their news sense acute, the story always just a subtle sniff away, and Peter has called Leni his 'Voice of Conscience', a valuable asset in the ethically choppy waters of true crime. But it was the sense of a story, that impulse of real journalists, which enabled them to uncover the duplicities within Truman Capote's true crime novella *Handcarved Coffins*, which led to their famous feature article 'Hoax: Secrets that Truman Capote Took to the Grave'.

The *Sunday Times* had ironically serialised *Handcarved Coffins* itself in Britain, and in the early 1990s, the paper sanctioned the

Gillman's investigation. Peter Gillman travelled to Holcomb, Kansas, the setting of Capote's *In Cold Blood*, reasoning that the Kansas Bureau of Investigation detective Al Dewey, who had helped Capote fill in the blanks on that book, might have an insight into the crimes described in *Handcarved Coffins* – a string of nasty murders, including by rattlesnake, burning to death in a basement and decapitation by tripwire, all of the victims having received a handmade miniature wooden coffin prior to their deaths. The heavily suspected but never convicted culprit was a menacing rancher named Quinn, whom Capote claimed in his book to have met.

But Al Dewey was dead, so Gillman had to do the next best thing and speak to his widow. After gaining her trust, a skill in itself in the small-town Midwest, as Capote himself had had to do decades earlier, Gillman began to realise that the story had real yet restless legs, and what followed was a master-class in investigative journalism, tracing Capote's movements, and trying to track down the said crimes, as well as the elusive Quinn. Capote had, in fact, used some real unconnected murders, but added his own other gruesome murders and details, invented the sole perpetrator Quinn, his detective character Jake Pepper (whom Gillman reveals was based on Al Dewey himself) and the eponymous handcarved coffins of the novella's title. Worst of all, 'Hoax' exposes the fact that Al Dewey had been planning his own book, based around real murders he had investigated. Capote had included details of a couple of these murders in the fictional string of homicides committed by the imaginary Quinn, but Capote had ruthlessly stolen his friend Dewey's idea, Dewey having asked him advice about his proposed book years earlier.

'Hoax' is written in a highly evocative and enticing style, which Capote, Gillman's quarry, would surely have appreciated. The opening doesn't begin in Kansas or the novella's setting of Nebraska, however, but in a publishing office in metropolitan New York: 'Joe Fox was astounded. On his desk, this late autumn day in 1979, was a manuscript bearing the name of Truman Capote. Two months before, Capote had promised Fox a "surprise", but Fox had been unimpressed: as Capote's long-suffering editor at the New York publishing company, Random House, he had grown weary of his endless promises. Now, Capote had delivered a manuscript to rank with his masterpiece, *In Cold Blood*.' Compare that story-framing device to the Gillman's description of his arrival in the Midwest town of Ensign, where one of the real murders investigated by Al Dewey, and purloined by Capote, had taken place: 'Ensign, as I found when I drove there on Highway 56 from Garden City, can justifiably be described – in Capote's words – as little and forlorn. A lowering grain elevator stands beside the highway and the gleaming tracks of the Santa Fe railroad. There is a farming equipment store, a taxidermist's shop, a tiny restaurant named Our Cafe and little else.'

'Hoax' invented a true crime subgenre – a true crime writer's investigation of another true crime writer's investigation and retelling of a crime. That original true crime writer's reputation must fall, if the investigation of that writer reveals untruths, because true crime, as we have noted, is defined as 'a genre where real crimes are examined and portrayed'. And they come no loftier in true crime reputation than Capote, and such a move was both brave and sensational. Capote had failed on both counts, and

Handcarved Coffins, while superbly written and imagined, is actually crime fiction. And as Capote had subtitled it 'A Non-Fiction Account of an American Crime', he had been deeply dishonest to his readers and publishers.

In 2005 Peter and Leni Gillman secured another true crime exclusive when they built up a correspondence with the late infamous child serial murderer Ian Brady, who along with his accomplice Myra Hindley, had become known as the Moors Murderers on their arrest in the mid-1960s, as they had buried all their victims, except the last, on desolate moors just outside Manchester in England. For the first time, Brady opened up about his childhood, saying, 'I had a very happy childhood free of fear ... I have no excuses.' The level of detail that the notoriously tricky, crafty, sociopathic Brady gave over is very surprising. For the first time myths about his early years were debunked, and new, true facts added, creating a far clearer picture of a very twisted and manipulative man.

Three years later Peter and Leni Gillman published 'Harry Horse: The Man Who Loved His Wife to Death'. 'Harry Horse' was the pen name of a noted cartoonist, award-winning children's writer and illustrator named Richard Horne, who had published his work in many major newspapers, as well as magazines such as the *New Yorker*. In addition he was a musician and was, as the piece says, 'a polymath', although his greatest talent was as an artist. A fractured, compartmentalised personality who had an emotionally unstable childhood and complicated family relationships, the man known as Harry Horse found his stabilising anchor and wife in Mandy Williamson, meeting her on the remote Shetland Islands, on the far north coast of Scotland. But tragically, after living together as man and wife in Edinburgh and elsewhere, Mandy contracted the gradually debilitating multiple sclerosis, forcing a move back to Mandy's native Shetland Islands – the tiny island of West Burra specifically – to be close to her family. Harry Horse wasn't happy on the relatively desolate island, and Mandy's deterioration caused him a great deal of emotional pain and despair. But what came next was unexpected.

Peter and Leni Gillman open with 'Shetland, on the island of West Burra. A cemetery occupies a grassy slope in the loch-side settlement of Papil. Among the headstones is what appears to be a fresh grave cut into the turf. There is a pebble-shaped boulder engraved: "In loving memory of Richard, our brother and uncle." Below the cemetery, the grey surface of the loch is ruffled in the March wind; above, rain drifts across the bleak hillside. This place marks the end of what has been cast as a deeply poignant tale.'

That's writing of the highest order, bringing both the setting and the story into sharp relief, and as the piece unfolds, we learn of what happened with a growing sense of terror, disbelief and shock, but there are no cheap sensationalised tactics employed by the writers – 'the tale' is classically told and told superbly, Shakespearean in dimension and tragedy. Richard (Harry Horse) and Mandy had been found dead in their cottage, the official announcement by the Scottish authorities being a double suicide pact. That's why Peter and Leni Gillman went to West Burra, to write a feature article about a tragic love-death pact.

But they soon realised that it was no agreed suicide made out of love, and began to investigate, through official channels and by interviewing people who knew the couple on the island, attempting to speak to Mandy's parents, and interviewing Richard's sisters and mother too in England. Richard had stabbed Mandy to death and then himself, including extreme self-mutilation. And it hadn't been a peaceful, quick passing – they had both bled to death, the crime scene, as the piece relays, absolutely horrific. Richard had psychologically disintegrated, and as the title of the article says, the death destruction he wreaked was one born of love and despair at the flickering out of that light.

It was a brave and tenacious investigation, using skills honed by Peter and Leni Gillman over decades, and they revealed to the world the terrible truth, which had been quietly hidden officially. That is what true crime, or any good journalism, is supposed to do. It was a real exclusive and, importantly due to the subject matter, the story is beautifully and sensitively told. 'Harry Horse: The Man Who Loved His Wife to Death' is a perfectly-formed masterpiece, the best true crime feature article ever written, full stop, or as the Americans say, period.

LUDOVIC KENNEDY
Key Works
Ten Rillington Place (book) 1961
The Airman and the Carpenter (book) 1985
Thirty-Six Murders and Two Immoral Earnings (book) 2003

Although Kennedy's breakthrough venture into true crime *Ten Rillington Place* was published almost half a decade before Capote's *In Cold Blood*, that benchmark which defines the modern period, it deserves to be included here, as it created a very important subgenre of true crime, that which focuses on miscarriages of justice.

The book examines the depraved murders of multiple women, including his wife, of the British serial killer John Christie at his house, at the now infamous London address of No 10 Rillington Place, in the 1940s and early 1950s. This had led to the execution by hanging of one of Christie's former tenants, the almost illiterate Timothy Evans, for the murders of his own wife and baby in that house, three years before Christie was hanged for the murders of Evans's wife, amongst many other murders, and was one of the great, indeed fateful, injustices ever carried out under British law.

Kennedy expertly details the whole story, in a driving and atmospheric narrative, bringing the seedy house, occupants and unfortunate one-time visitors to life, having done copious research during his investigation, and the celebrated Foreword to the book implored the British government to look again at Evans's case, and give him a posthumous pardon. Its publication led to a furore in the media, other books and journalism, and Evans's pardon in 1966, as well as adding to the call to abolish the death penalty in Britain, which followed in 1969, although the last hangings took place in 1964. That's quite an important contribution to both justice and true crime.

Almost twenty-five years later, having written other books on various subjects, Kennedy published *The Airman and the Carpenter*, this time looking at one of the biggest crime cases of the American twentieth century, the kidnapping and murder of the celebrated aviator Charles Lindbergh's baby, for which the German immigrant Richard 'Bruno' Hauptmann was executed in 1936. Kennedy took the view that Hauptmann had been neither the kidnapper nor killer, and again his campaigning research was thorough and writing succinct and thought-provoking, although opinion is still divided on whether Hauptmann was guilty or not.

In *Thirty-Six Murders and Two Immoral Earnings*, Kennedy analysed other infamous miscarriage cases, such as the hounding of Stephen Ward during the Profumo political crisis of the early 1960s, Derek Bentley who was hanged under the law of Joint Enterprise and much later also pardoned, and the Birmingham Six, the six innocent men who were convicted and served long sentences for IRA pub bombings, which caused many fatalities, in the early 1970s in that city. Although he was by now very much a member of 'the Establishment', and had been knighted by the Queen, Kennedy was scathing about the centuries-old British legal system in that book.

Since Kennedy took up the miscarriage of justice mantle, having inherited it himself from earlier practitioners such as his fellow Scot William Roughead, other important writers and journalists – and film documentary makers, such as Errol Morris, whose 1988 *The Thin Blue Line* is a true crime miscarriage masterpiece about corruption in the Texas justice system – have worked in this area of true crime. Paul Foot, who died in 2004, was a leading investigative journalist, and looked deeply into the 'Bridgewater Four' – four men convicted of the murder of a schoolboy named Carl Bridgewater – both in journalism and in his 1986 book *Murder at the Farm: Who Killed Carl Bridgewater?* In 1997 the four men were exonerated and finally released from prison, although one had died inside. Foot had also been a long-time campaigner for the clearing of the name of the executed James Hanratty in 1962, who had been convicted of shooting and killing Michael Gregsten and raping, paralysing and leaving for dead Gregsten's lover Valerie Storie in what was known in Britain as 'the A6 Layby Murder', due to the slip road on which it occurred. Foot's articles and book on the case, along with high-profile Ludovic Kennedy's involvement, kept the case alive for years.

Bob Woffinden, originally a music journalist, turned to true crime miscarriage of justice reporting and documentary-making in the 1980s, publishing his landmark book *Miscarriages of Justice* in 1989, which examined a wide variety of British 'miscarriage' cases over many years. Written fluently, and highly readable, with a real sense and grasp of detail and rational argument, the book is a tornado of injustice that slowly builds, by the end engulfing you. Later he turned to the case of Hanratty too, with 1999's *Hanratty: The Final Verdict*, an expert dissection of the case, which lays all the facts out concisely in one place for the first time. This helped lead to the retesting of an item of clothing from the crime scene in 2001, on which Hanratty's DNA was found, leading to the Court of Appeal stating that Hanratty's guilt was proved beyond doubt. While Foot and Woffinden said that it was a case of evidential cross-contamination, Kennedy accepted the finding and said so in *Thirty-Six Murders and Two Immoral Earnings*. Bob Woffinden, who died in April 2018, produced work over a long career which supported the accused and convicted in key cases and led to changes in British law. He cast much-needed light on miscarriages of justice, not always those involving murder, but all kinds of cases, as can be seen in his 2016 book *The Nicholas Cases*.

Writers such as Ludovic Kennedy, Paul Foot and Bob Woffinden are a rare breed, and the work they do takes great faith, self-belief and emotional investment, as well as an analytical and tenacious mind, and above all real determination. But it is extremely important work – the most vital in the true crime genre as it can, and does, still affect real people's lives in absolute ways.

NORMAN MAILER
Key Works
The Executioner's Song (book) 1979

Much to the chagrin of Truman Capote, his professional rival Norman Mailer's only venture into true crime, the gargantuan (some would say overlong) almost 1100-page *The Executioner's Song* won a prestigious 1980 Pulitzer Prize, while Capote's *In Cold Blood* had not. At the time that Capote's watershed book was first read in 1965-66, Mailer, who had made his name as a novelist before writing some non-fiction in parallel, had said that this new non-fiction novel genre was 'a failure of imagination'. Mailer had also failed to publicly credit the influence of *In Cold Blood* in persuading him to enter the genre, but later said that he hadn't as comparisons between the two books were so obvious that any words would be superfluous.

Capote got his revenge in the Foreword to his 1980 book *Music For Chameleons* saying somewhat passively-aggressively – Capote could often be bitchy and actively aggressive – that Mailer was 'a good writer and a fine fellow and I'm grateful to have been some small service to him.' It seems too coincidental that Capote's *Handcarved Coffins* appeared in the same year as *The Executioner's Song*, and it is entirely possible that Capote knew that Mailer, probably his greatest professional rival, was about to make a media and critical splash in the genre. The irrepressible Mailer always made a big splash, and his new work in the genre, the first in almost fifteen years, was his riposte.

In fact, *The Executioner's Song* and *In Cold Blood* are very different kinds of books. Firstly, Mailer didn't do the personal lengthy groundwork research that Capote had done, but employed two full-time researchers to amass a huge amount of information about Gary Gilmore, the protagonist of *The Executioner's Song*, his damaged life, the needless murders he had committed, and above all his fight to be executed. That latter theme was the major one in Mailer's opus: an examination of Gilmore's struggle, over years on Death Row, to be executed, while every other prisoner was doing everything they could to avoid or delay that final state punishment. Capote scoffed in an interview that Mailer hadn't got truly involved in his subject, as he had, and that is true, but he still had to write the book.

Secondly, Mailer termed *The Executioner's Song* 'A Novel', which gave him far more artistic scope, although the book has always been considered as a work of true crime. Mailer doesn't have Capote's gorgeous prose style, but he is a vitally clean, subtle and concise writer, who is able to offer deep psychological and sociological insights, or informed speculation, often profound, into Gilmore's mind, background and his extreme predicament. This is Mailer struggling to rationalise Gilmore's death wish, 'for some persons at some times, it is rational not to avoid physical death at all costs. Indeed the spark of humanity can maximize its essence by choosing an alternative that preserves the greatest dignity and some tranquillity of mind.' While Capote's style washes over you in tidal waves of sheer power, Mailer's is cumulative and laps and creeps up on you – in American literary lineage Capote being more of the F. Scott Fitzgerald school and Mailer that of Ernest Hemingway.

Gilmore was a cold-blooded murderer, but Mailer has some sympathy for him, Gilmore having felt remorse over time, and then finding peace and reaching an acceptance of his own death: 'Then the Warden said, "Do you have anything you'd like to say?" and Gary looked up at the ceiling and hesitated, then said, "Let's do it." That was it.' Just as Hemingway had a preoccupation with the human condition, masculinity and courage, Mailer finds courage, masculinity and humanity in Gary Gilmore, and for that, as well as the expert reportage and microscopically detailed recreation of Gilmore's alien world (with the qualification that it could have been better edited and a more compact work) *The Executioner's Song* is one of the very best true crime books ever written.

JANET MALCOLM
Key Works
The Journalist and the Murderer (two-part serialisation in the *New Yorker* March-April, 1989); (book) 1990

Janet Malcolm is a highly accomplished writer with an absolutely first-class intellect who has written seminal books on psychoanalysis and Freud's theories. In *The Journalist and the Murderer* she tackled one of the biggest ethical concerns facing the true crime writer – the nature of the relationship between author and subject in collaboration, and the ethical and professional limits of that close contact. The book has another of the great openings in true crime, which is enough to get the reader, and especially journalists, immediately thinking and questioning themselves: 'Any journalist who is not too stupid or too full of himself to notice what is going on knows that what he is doing is morally indefensible. He is a kind of confidence man, preying on people's vanity, ignorance, or loneliness, gaining their trust and betraying them without remorse.'

The focus of Malcolm's book is the relationship between the bestselling non-fiction writer Joe McGinniss and Jeffrey MacDonald, soon to be convicted of the 1970 murders of his pregnant wife and two young daughters. Malcolm unravels the development of that author-subject connection, and reveals, through letters that McGinniss sent MacDonald over several years, in and out of prison, that McGinniss had inveigled himself into MacDonald's confidence to get him to open up. It worked, and McGinniss gained access to as much of the detached MacDonald's mind as was psychologically possible for him, or at least as much of it that he wanted to give over without incriminating himself, if indeed he was his family's killer. There is also an intruder theory, which too has strong evidence, favoured by MacDonald's defence teams from the trial's numerous appeals, and his supporters. McGinniss was also able to peruse MacDonald's voluminous case files and personal archive in MacDonald's home office, and was even allowed to sit in and go behind the scenes with MacDonald and his legal team at length.

Soon, as Malcolm shows, McGinniss and MacDonald were 'friends', and MacDonald deeply trusted the writer, who had promised him and his case a fair and honest portrayal in the finished book, and made it clear in letters that he believed in

MacDonald's innocence – that is until he didn't need access to him anymore, as Malcolm alleges. But when McGinniss's book *Fatal Vision* came out, becoming a huge bestseller and causing a sensation in 1983, MacDonald was shocked to discover that McGinniss had shown him as guilty of the murder of his family while on amphetamines, and saying that as author he'd come to realise after going over all the evidence again and again that MacDonald was guilty of the multiple murders of his wife and children. Unfortunately, McGinniss had never told MacDonald of this change of heart. MacDonald later won a civil suit against McGinniss, with the author settling out of court, and the true crime writer Joseph Wambaugh, also profiled on p. 90 of this book, was one of the writers who gave evidence in McGinniss's defence.

The Journalist and the Murderer is a hugely important book, and Janet Malcolm, through stringent intellectual argument and interviews with all the main players in the affair – McGinniss, MacDonald, his legal team, the jurors and expert witnesses – brings the debate of the ethics of author–subject collaboration into the open. This is unresolvable in an absolute way, as the levels of ethics expected in this situation vary from writer to writer, but reading Malcolm's book certainly reminds true crime writers particularly of the ethical concerns of their trade.

BRIAN MASTERS
Key Works
Killing For Company: The Story of a Man Addicted to Murder (book) 1985

Brian Masters is a major true crime writer who had to take a great deal of care when researching and writing his masterpiece, *Killing*

For Company, for which he collaborated closely with the London serial killer Dennis Nilsen, who cold-bloodedly strangled and dismembered fifteen young men and attempted to kill others in the space of four years. The book also has one of the great true crime titles, as indeed, as Masters's book conveys clearly, Nilsen couldn't bear to lose the men who stayed the night at the two addresses where he lived and by murdering them, in his detached and abnormal mind, he had their company forever.

Masters had already written critical books about French literature and non-fiction books about the British aristocracy, and would go on to write *The Shrine of Jeffrey Dahmer* (1993), perhaps America's answer to Dennis Nilsen, although it certainly never asked for one, and *'She Must Have Known': The Trial of Rosemary West* (1996), which preceded Gordon Burn's definitive book on the Fred and Rose West case, *Happy Like Murderers*, by two years. Brian Masters broke true crime ground with *Killing For Company*. The level of access that he had to Nilsen's thoughts post-arrest was unprecedented, and the way that he delivered his examination of Nilsen's life, alienation, mind-set, terrible murders and his reasoning after conviction may never be surpassed, as very few killers of the macabre magnitude of Nilsen ever speak on-the-record, and when they do, they rarely give much real insight into their actions.

Nilsen shared poems, daily, sometimes twice-daily letters at the peak of their relationship, and his inner thoughts with Masters, and the author very skilfully filled in the gaps of Nilsen's life from the beginning in Aberdeenshire, Scotland, right through to 1983, when he was working as a civil servant in an employment centre by day, and killing at night at weekends, until he was arrested at his north London flat, when human flesh had been found in the house's drains, Nilsen having flushed pieces of dismembered tissue down the toilet, the police finding bagged body parts in his wardrobe, and a human head on his oven hob in a saucepan, having been boiled. There is no way to avoid these details, Masters certainly didn't – and to understand the scope of Masters's achievement one has to be fully aware of the depths of Nilsen's abnormality.

Several years before Janet Malcolm published *The Journalist and the Murderer*, Masters honestly questioned himself and his relationship with Nilsen, who was in prison awaiting trial, in the narrative of *Killing For Company*: 'Throughout this tempestuous time, his relationship with me gradually developed into real loyalty … I imagined also that he might be a clever manipulator using me for his own ends; he could not have escaped detection for four years without some native cunning. I was now fast becoming his mouthpiece, his only contact with the outside world, and I should not underestimate his ability to engineer situations which might make me his moral representative.' Indeed, Masters did come in for some criticism upon publication from some who said that he had humanised Nilsen and sympathised with him too much. But this is surely unfair – Masters is scrupulously honest and balanced, as much as he can be, about Nilsen throughout the book.

There are also some real insights into the reality of a psychologically alienated mind such as Nilsen's, and the way that he presented himself to the outside world, and may explain how he managed to pick up his victims in pubs and bars, men who trusted him enough to accept his invitation to go back to his flat.

Here's Masters on his first face-to-face meeting with Nilsen in prison: 'From the letters already exchanged, I expected a sensitive and introspective man. At our first meeting we sat opposite one another across a small table, and I saw an assertive man, bristling with confidence and swagger, amazingly relaxed ... '

Killing For Company is by far the best and the most penetrating true crime book ever written with real access to a killer.

ANN RULE
Key Works
The Stranger Beside Me (book) 1980

'As a professional writer, I have been handed the story of a lifetime, a story any author prays for,' wrote the from-then-on prolific Ann Rule in the Preface to her first and best book, *The Stranger Beside Me*. Unique in true crime, Rule had known Ted Bundy, one of the most infamous, dangerous and menacingly enigmatic serial killers ever, the killer of at least thirty-eight young women, *before* his crime spree began. While working as a true crime magazine writer, she began to follow the story of the string of murders in the early to mid 1970s, across different American states, working closely with her excellent police contacts, not knowing that her ex-colleague, the preppy, highly intelligent, impeccably polite and handsome Bundy was the culprit.

They worked together as call operators in a crisis centre, Rule working night shifts as a volunteer, Bundy on a paid graduate programme. They got to know each other over those long hours, between dealing with, helping and sometimes saving the lives of troubled and suicidal callers. She opened up to Ted, and he to her.

They attended parties together with other friends, despite the fact that she was fifteen years older than him. It was a purely platonic friendship, but one with an emotional connection.

Only a little later, when Rule and Bundy were no longer in regular contact after she left the crisis centre, as evidence pointing to the culprit begin to mount – when he was overheard trying to pick up a victim and saying his name was Ted, the photo-fit drawn up by the police for the media looked like her old friend, and it became known that the killer tried to lure women to his Volkswagen Beetle – did Rule check to see if Bundy, whom she hadn't seen for almost a year, drove a VW Beetle. A police friend checked, and found that he did. This troubled Rule, but the information was filed with hundreds of other leads and never followed up until much later, and Rule, thinking that she was being over-suspicious about her old friend Ted, banished the thought from her mind.

There's little wonder that Rule at that point thought it was just too incredible. Bundy had a girlfriend, was attractive to women, conservatively dressed in that hippie era, had never shown any violence or aggression in front of her, he had a bright future career in either law or political administration, and in fact would be a son-in-law that any parent would be proud to accept into their family. This is how Rule describes Bundy the first time she met him at the crisis centre: 'He looked up and grinned. He was twenty-four then ... I liked him immediately. It would have been hard not to ... He was one of those rare people who listen with full attention, who evince a genuine caring by their very stance. You could tell things to Ted that you might never tell anyone else.' Within two years, Ted Bundy would be abducting, raping and murdering women, often pretending he needed help, with his arm or leg in a fake plaster cast, to get young women to assist him and come to his car.

The book builds a full portrait of Bundy, and that personal knowledge of Bundy, before he was arrested, is invaluable, and it is frightening how plausible, in fact downright disarming, that Bundy, a manipulative and cunning psychopath and sociopath, was. But then again, that's why those young women who became his prey went with him – save for one or two who had lucky escapes: one young woman he approached told police that she was going to help him carry something to his car, but then she was terrified when his eyes changed, becoming staring and manic. Was this the predator inside him emerging from the smooth and 'normal' exterior that he presented to everybody, including Ann Rule? We go on a long journey of realisation and disbelief with Rule, as she learns the horrible truth, before the public did, as she had remarkable access to the police investigation. The full horrors of Ted Bundy's despicable, heartless crimes slowly emerge, in a slow-burning and building narrative, written in a personal and intimate style, with Rule our narrator, using the authorial 'I'. *The Killer Beside Me* is a unique true crime book.

GITTA SERENY
Key Works
The Case of Mary Bell: A Portrait of a Child Who Murdered (book) 1972
Cries Unheard: Why Children Kill – The Story of Mary Bell (book) 1998

The tragic murders and mutilation of two toddlers on a Newcastle housing estate in northeast England in 1968 shocked the local community, and when it was discovered that the killer was an exceptionally pretty ten-year-old girl named Mary Bell, a fellow resident on that estate, the whole of Britain and the world was stunned. Bell became known as 'The Devil Child' in the media, and when she was convicted, everybody breathed a sigh of relief. This dangerous child was off the streets, and most felt that she had been born evil and good riddance to her, the two poor little boys she had killed and their grieving families justifiably getting enormous sympathy. But it was a classic case of nature versus nurture – had Mary Bell been born murderous, or had the environment that she had been brought up in made her that way? The public knee-jerk reaction, shared by the majority of the authorities and court experts was that Bell was inherently evil. But the writer Gitta Sereny suspected very differently, and her two books on the Mary Bell case, published twenty-six years apart, tell the real story.

There's no doubt that what Bell did was wicked, and other actions, which were splashed across the tabloid media after her conviction were deeply troubling. The graffiti that she and a young friend (who was often with her, but not an accomplice in murder) left around, with menacing threats, a mixture of misspelt child-speak and swear words, and the chilling note 'I murder SO that I come back' were like something from a horror film, as was the fact that after murdering one of the boys, Mary Bell knocked on the door of her victim's house on the day of his funeral, asking to see him, and when his traumatised mother gently told her that he was dead, Mary Bell reportedly said that she knew that, but wanted to see him in his coffin, which was laid out in the house. Was this behaviour incredibly psychologically damaged or just plain bad? What Sereny did in her first book on the case, having attended the trial and watched Mary closely, explored the housing estate and interviewed Bell's family and key local people, was show that the former was true, and that Bell was playing games in her mind, having detached herself from reality to numb herself from the pain of her upbringing.

Sereny had been jointly interested in the darker side of human nature and child emotional development for many years: she had attended the Nuremberg trials in 1945 as an observer, where she saw Hitler's architect Albert Speer, about whom she would later write an incredible book called *Albert Speer: His Battle With Truth*, and after the Second World War she worked for the United Nations Relief and Rehabilitation Administration, helping to reunite children kidnapped by the Nazis with their birth parents. So when she approached the case of Mary Bell as a writer, she was well-equipped. *The Case of Mary Bell: A Portrait of a Child Who Murdered* was a major book when it appeared in 1972, just four years after the murders, and showed Sereny to have an acute emotional and intellectual intelligence, just what the subject required.

But it was her second book on the case *Cries Unheard: Why Children Kill – The Story of Mary Bell* which really explained everything about the case. It goes into far more detail about the case, Mary Bell having since been released from incarceration, where she was treated inappropriately by the authorities, as she was such a rare prisoner, and Bell's troubles before she was released with a new identity to a secret location are detailed. But above all,

Sereny worked with Bell on the book, and even gave her a share of the advance, which caused uproar when it was revealed in the media. Ethically, it was a very tricky collaboration, and made much worse by the intense media scrutiny on Mary Bell, newspapers attacking both Bell and Sereny. Sereny herself writes, 'This secrecy, not only about Mary's whereabouts, but about the whole project, was to become a heavy load for both Mary and me.'

The resultant book was well worth it however, and gives us the only really penetrating insight written into the development and causal motivations of a child who murders. Bell had been terribly physically neglected and physically, sexually and emotionally abused from a startlingly young age, and the details which Sereny starkly yet sensitively relays in Part Five of the book, entitled 'Return to Childhood 1957 to 1968', are extremely unsettling. Mary Bell told Sereny how her late mother, who was a prostitute, 'pimped' her out in their house to local men from the age of seven or eight. By the time that she became a double murderer aged ten, Mary Bell was a psychological wreck, having become sociopathic to survive.

Both books should be read together, in chronological order as companion pieces, so by the end of *Cries Unheard*, the reader has a far clearer understanding of Mary Bell. Her crimes were horrific, but then so was her treatment as a child. Sereny's books on Mary Bell are two of the most psychologically important true crime books ever written.

JOSEPH WAMBAUGH
Key Works
The Onion Field (book) 1973

Joseph Wambaugh is far from being the only former policeman to write true crime – the personal work experience of course gives a perfect insight into the subject. Once a Sergeant in the Los Angeles Police Department, Wambaugh has written many bestselling true crime books, even one set in Britain, about the killer Colin Pitchfork, who was the first murderer caught by DNA in the 1980s. But *The Onion Field*, his third book and first in the true crime genre, is Wambaugh's masterpiece.

Set in 1963, it tells the true story of two LAPD plainclothes police officers Karl Hettinger and Ian Campbell, who made a routine traffic stop of a suspicious car in Hollywood, and how the criminals inside it kidnapped the officers, taking them to the onion field of the book's title, where 31-year-old Ian Campbell was shot in the mouth and killed, with 28-year-old Hettinger managing to escape. The reasoning for the murder was that the criminals, Jimmy Lee Smith, alias Youngblood, and Gregory Powell (Campbell's killer, whom Wambaugh later interviewed in prison), thought that kidnapping, which they had already committed, was a capital crime, and capital crimes carried an automatic death sentence in California at that time. They thought that killing the witnesses to the kidnapping, the victims themselves, was the best option. But they were wrong – kidnapping was only a capital crime in California if the kidnap victim was harmed.

Wambaugh's knowledge of police work within the LAPD, and the risks that officers took daily, is evocatively brought to life in

The Onion Field. We are in the hands of a writer who intricately knows that world, how it feels. The fear is ramping up as we invest emotionally in the two officers. But the crime and its immediate aftermath and consequences and the arrests and trials of the perpetrators are only part of the book. There is also the treatment of the survivor Karl Hettinger when he returns to duty. As well as feeling guilty about his partner's murder and his escape, Hettinger was ostracised and bullied by other police officers, and less than three years after the kidnapping and Campbell's murder, Hettinger was accused of shoplifting, and had to resign from the LAPD. The murdered Ian Campbell, meanwhile, became a hero, within the force and the wider community.

Wambaugh brings the world within the LAPD to life. He is incredibly honest about the police officers he portrays, and they are human, with flaws like the rest of us. We become part of that world while reading, sympathy for both Ian Campbell, and then Karl Hettinger, engulf us and then make us feel conflicted. Both men were victims. Campbell paid with his life and Hettinger with his self-respect and career. It's a truly masterly book, thought-provoking, and with great subtlety in both characterisation and narrative.

CONCLUSION

WE ALL KNOW THAT BAD, SOMETIMES terrible, things happen to good people, and that there are no moral certainties in our world, there never have been, and never will be, unless we go down the dangerous path of genetic manipulation, brainwashing – mass censorship, or drugging, as predicted by George Orwell in *1984* with 'doublethink' and the Thought Police, and Aldous Huxley with the drug soma in *Brave New World* – although some may think that the social media homogenisation of our societies is already halfway down that road. In both dystopian visions, human thought, and therefore freedom, is curtailed. We don't live in a truly dystopian world yet, thankfully, but it is far from perfect, as flawed as the people within it.

Human beings are complex: our brains use about 20 per cent of our bodies' energy, and we understand not nearly enough about what our brains can do. Our brains control our actions unless we are lobotomized, and those actions are both good and bad. We are wise to be aware of that, and to remember it. Where there is normality there is also abnormality, light there is shade, sun there is shadow. To return to Orwell's 'doublethink', we don't want to use logic against logic to arrive at our conclusions, and hide from the truth, but use our logic to comprehend ourselves and our world better. And to do that, we need to confront that shade, shadow, and sometimes what seems like total darkness. That's what will make us better as a race and our lives safer and happier.

True crime writing exposes and faces that darkness, and the various levels of gloom, nightmare and depravity amongst us – digging for the truth, whether injustice, corruption, organised or violent criminality, mining misery and traversing tragedy to reach a deeper level of awareness, see the rats under the ground of our well-kept streets. We may never know all the answers, but if we don't try we must live in ignorance, and without the power that is knowledge, greater pain. Most people have a natural curiosity to learn, to push the boundaries of their knowledge, and fascination with the macabre and nightmarish is a human trait, especially within creative imaginations.

But we must always keep perspective, remain positive yet discerning, and use our greater understanding of each other to move forward. Psychopaths and sociopaths do walk with us every day, it's a fact, and many of us show some of those tendencies at times. The vast majority would rather not think about it in reality, and when reading about and watching such extreme personalities, there is some comfort in our mundane lives, where we can go back to suspending disbelief, as we sit in warmth, instead of ending up in that field, alleyway, or strange room. The shock is momentary or temporary.

There is also the innate human impulse for justice. Most of us want to see wrongs prevented, or at least righted. When we see a perpetrator exposed and punished, it gives us faith once again in the quest for the ideal natural order of things, whether by dogged investigation, using positive brain power to defeat the negative, or just a sense of karma. The seeking of justice and the punishment of injustice leads to a sense of redemption, even among the most jaded or cynical. Over centuries, as well as taking us into that darkness, the best true crime writing has fed that need, delivered some small sense of redemption, given back some faith in our world and therefore ourselves and humanity as a species, especially when we can understand that most crimes happen for a reason, psychologically or sociologically, or both.

When the prolific American bank robber Willie Sutton was asked why he robbed banks, he replied that it was because there was money in them. When the mountaineer George Mallory was asked by a *New York Times* reporter in 1923 why he continued risking his life trying to reach the summit of Mount Everest, he replied that it was because it was there. People write and read about true crime because there is darkness there, whether lived in by individuals or subcultures, and our logic tells us that we ignore it at our peril – it may sometimes be uncomfortable, even for the most seasoned, but at least we can try to brave it, intellectually and psychologically grasp it, and perhaps even empathise with it.

Bibliography

MODERN MASTERS

BRESLIN, JIMMY

'Son of Sam', *New York Daily News*, 5 June 1977; *The Mammoth Book of Murder*, Carroll & Graf, 1989

The Good Rat, Mainstream Publishing, Edinburgh, 2008

BURN, GORDON

Somebody's Husband, Somebody's Son, William Heinemann, London, 1984

Happy Like Murderers, Faber & Faber, London, 1998

The Trial, *Granta* magazine, April 1996

CAMPBELL, DUNCAN

That Was Business, This Is Personal, Secker & Warburg, London, 1990

The Underworld, BBC Books, 1994

A Stranger and Afraid: The Story of Caroline Beale, Macmillan, 1997

We'll All Be Murdered in Our Beds! The Shocking History of Crime Reporting in Britain, Elliott & Thompson, London, 2016

CAPOTE, TRUMAN

In Cold Blood, Penguin Classics, 2000

Handcarved Coffins, included in *Music For Chameleons*, Abacus, London, 1987

CARRÈRE, EMMANUEL

The Adversary: A True Story of Monstrous Deception (translated by Linda Coverdale), Bloomsbury, London 2001

DUNNE, DOMINICK

Justice: Crimes, Trials & Punishments, Sphere, 2001

GILLMAN, PETER & LENI

'Hoax: Secrets that Truman Capote Took to the Grave', *Sunday Times Magazine,* 21 June 1992

'Exclusive: Moors Murderer Ian Brady's Childhood', *Mail on Sunday,* 15 May 2005

'Harry Horse: The Man Who Loved His Wife to Death', *Sunday Times,* 13 July 2008

KENNEDY, LUDOVIC

Ten Rillington Place, HarperCollins, London, 1996

The Airman and the Carpenter: The Lindbergh Kidnapping and the Framing of Richard Hauptmann, HarperCollins, London, 1985

Thirty-Six Murders and Two Immoral Earnings, Profile Books, London, 2003

MAILER, NORMAN

The Executioner's Song, Vintage Classics, 1989

MALCOLM, JANET

The Journalist and the Murderer, Bloomsbury, London, 1991

MASTERS, BRIAN

Killing For Company: The Story of a Man Addicted to Murder, Jonathan Cape, London, 1985

ANN RULE

The Stranger Beside Me, Sphere, 2013

GITTA SERENY

The Case of Mary Bell: A Portrait of a Child Who Murdered, Methuen, 1972

Cries Unheard: Why Children Kill – The Story of Mary Bell, Macmillan, 1998

JOSEPH WAMBAUGH

The Onion Field, Quercus, 2008

GENERAL ARTICLES & BOOKS

Fox, Lorna Scott, 'There Will Always Be Blood: True Crime Writing', the *Nation,* March 2009

Grobel, Lawrence, *Conversations with Capote,* Da Capo Press, 2000

Linderman, Eric, 'Criminal Broadsides of 19th-Century England', Kent State University, 1997

McCrum, Robert, 'An Introduction to *The Moonstone*', British Library website, 15 May 2014

Oates, Joyce Carol, 'The Mystery of JonBenét Ramsey', *New York Review of Books* Vol. 46, No. 11, 24 June 1999

Richter, David, *True Crime in Nineteenth-Century Literature,* Queen's College, New York

Schechter, Harold, *True Crime: An American Anthology,* The Library of America, 2008

OTHER TITLES OF INTEREST

POETRY IN EXILE

A Study of the Poetry of Auden, Brodsky & Szirtes

Michael Murphy

978-1-871551-76-1 (pbk) 270pp

DEREK MAHON

A Study of His Poetry

Christopher Steare

978-1-910996-08-9 (pbk) 232pp

BETWEEN TWO WORLDS

A Survey of Writing in Britain, 1900-1914

Hugh Underhill

978-1-906075-55-2 (pbk) 188pp

To find out more about these and other titles visit

www.greenex.co.uk